Douglas Globemaster II

Long Beach's Long Reach

BOB ARCHER

HISTORIC MILITARY AIRCRAFT SERIES, VOLUME 36

Front cover image: Three 63rd Troop Carrier Wing (TCW) C-124Cs painted in the most flamboyant color scheme, featuring Day-Glo orange applied to the nose, rear fuselage and wing tip heater. Sadly, the bright orange was gone by 1963. Seen at Christchurch, New Zealand, during November 1961 while supporting Operation *Deep Freeze*. (Jack Friell collection)

Title page image: C-124s were always popular at UK air shows, as their cavernous cargo hold was so impressive when open to the public – it was also an ideal shelter when the fickle British weather turned unpleasant. 52-0950 of the 63rd TCW detachment at Rhein-Main Air Base (AB) is seen at Wethersfield in August 1964. (Phil Owen)

Contents page image: A very striking view of Oakland Airport, California, circa early 1958 with a pair of C-124s including 52-1078, as well as a Military Air Transport Service (MATS) C-97 and a number of Lockheed T-33 Shooting Stars receiving maintenance. The Aircraft Engineering and Maintenance Company carried out military overhauls for many years. (William T Larkins)

Back cover image: Experience of flying equipment into snow-covered airfields during construction of the Distant Early Warning Line within the Arctic Circle region of North America was the main reason the 63rd TCW was selected for Operation *Deep Freeze*. C-124C 52-1013 is seen at Fort Churchill, in 1956. (Bob Uebel)

This book is dedicated to all the C-124 aircrew who flew and ground crew
who supported Globemaster operations for 25 years.

Published by Key Books
An imprint of Key Publishing Ltd
PO Box 100
Stamford
Lincs PE9 1XQ

www.keypublishing.com

The right of Bob Archer to be identified as the author of this book has been asserted in accordance with the Copyright, Designs and Patents Act 1988 Sections 77 and 78.

Copyright © Bob Archer, 2023

ISBN 978 1 80282 595 4

Typeset by SJmagic DESIGN SERVICES, India.

Contents

Introduction

Personnel associated with the Douglas C-124 Globemaster II gave the aircraft a variety of nicknames. While some were slightly derogatory, none were intended to be offensive, and most were a term of affection in a tongue-in-cheek way. However, the generally used moniker was "Old Shakey," as the C-124 flew unpressurized, usually at an altitude of 10,000ft (3,048m), and was therefore subjected to the turbulence that higher-flying contemporaries were not. Another nickname was "a million rivets flying in loose formation," as the sheer size of the aircraft probably had this number of fixtures.

However, almost all aircrews and ground technicians loved the C-124, as the "old girl" most often arrived at its intended destinations, despite the all too habitual consequence of at least one of the unreliable Pratt & Whitney Wasp Major engines developing a technical issue and needing to be shut down. The "Globie" could often fly long distances on just three engines and, while unnerving for the crew at the time, usually reached safety where repairs could be affected. Furthermore, flight crews soon became familiar with the vibration caused by the four Wasp Majors producing an almost unique shudder throughout the entire airframe!

61st Military Airlift Wing (MAW) 52-1012 departing Hickam Air Force Base (AFB), Hawaii, shortly before being damaged at Mactan AB, Philippines, on August 8, 1967. Disposal of the aircraft was vested with the resident 463rd Tactical Air Wing (TAW), and following cannibalization for reusable parts, was struck off change (SOC) in November 1968. (Nick Williams)

The C-124 was the US military's answer to the requirement for an outsized airlifter that first became apparent during World War Two, when urgent supplies, including armor, needed to be transported over intercontinental ranges. Most large weaponry was delivered by sea, which was extremely vulnerable to enemy submarines. Therefore, the necessity for an airlifter that could span the Atlantic Ocean between the United States and Europe, with an acceptable payload, began to take shape. This was subsequently reinforced when the US and its allies outwitted the Soviet Union by resupplying the city of Berlin in 1948/1949 during the unprecedented Airlift.

The C-124 arrived at the right time, and created the link between the World War Two-era Douglas C-47 Skytrain and C-54 Skymaster, and the jet-powered airlifters of the 1960s, such as the Lockheed C-141 Starlifter. The Globie resembled a shoe box on end, with wings attached, and seemed so antiquated when parked alongside the sleek C-141. Nevertheless, both achieved their assigned goals, and both left a legacy along with fond memories for crews and enthusiasts alike. Indeed, former C-124 navigator and author Billy D Higgins has suggested that the aircraft went into the Vietnam War as a two-and-a-half-star airplane that produced five-star results. This was due in no small part to the people who operated and maintained the Globemaster, who exceeded all expectations.

Above: 53-0032 basks in the sun at Will Rogers World Airport, Oklahoma City, during August 1973. (Ron Monroe)

Right: 436th MAW C-124C 52-1055 about to have the tow bar connected after an event at Rhein-Main AB during 1968.

The Globemaster was equally at home on snow-packed airports near the Arctic Circle, as shown here at Fort Churchill, Manitoba, in April 1955, as it was in the heat of the Sahara Desert. 63rd TCW 52-0950 was supporting the Mid-Canada and Pinetree Early Warning Lines to protect North America from Soviet incursions. (63rd TCW Association)

52-1009 was detached from Hickam AFB to the 61st MAW at Tachikawa AB, Japan, during the second half of the 1960s. (Nick Williams)

Chapter 1

The Globemaster II

The Douglas Aircraft Company designed the C-74 Globemaster following a request by the US Army for an airlifter capable of delivering outsized loads and large volumes of cargo over intercontinental range. However, the end of World War Two curtailed many defense contracts, including that for a sizeable fleet of C-74s. Undeterred, Donald Douglas, president of the company, clearly understood that the progress of technology had rapidly overtaken the C-74 design and there was a need to increase the scale of the airlifter that the Army would need. Furthermore, the Berlin Airlift of 1948/1949 underlined the necessity for a larger transportation capability, which could be loaded and unloaded quickly.

YC-124

Using the fifth C-74A, serial 42-65406, as a pattern for a new aircraft model, the resulting aircraft, the YC-124, featured a fuselage doubled in size and accessed by folding ramps located behind massive clam shell doors.

The US Army Air Force had intended to buy a large fleet of C-74As, but World War Two ended before the type entered service. Therefore, just 14 were completed, and served only briefly with MATS. 42-65412 flew from Brookley AFB, Alabama, before retirement to the Military Aircraft Storage and Disposition Center (MASDC) on March 26, 1956. It was registered as N3183G for the Pan American Bank of Miami and flown to Long Beach for storage, where this photograph was taken, then eventually abandoned and later scrapped. (William T Larkins)

This YC-124 has allocated serial 42-65406 but is carrying only the buzz number CA406 on the tail. CA was the buzz number identity for the C-124, although no other Globemasters were allocated this form of identification. This aircraft is seen shortly after roll out at Long Beach, California. Applied to the nose wheel doors is the planned first flight date of November 26, 1949. The aircraft lacks any unit insignia, as it was initially retained by Douglas for evaluation. (Douglas)

After a period of testing by the manufacturer and the United States Air Force (USAF), YC-124 42-65406 was assigned to the San Antonio Air Materiel Area, and eventually retired to the Air Force Museum at Wright-Patterson AFB, Ohio. However, when the exhibits were relocated to their present site, the C-124 was too large to move, and was eventually scrapped. It is seen in June 1968. (Steve Miller)

Designated as the YC-124, the prototype emerged from the Long Beach, California, plant in November 1949, and was retained by the company for evaluation before undergoing further testing with various United States Air Force (USAF) research organisations. This included assessment at Edwards Air Force Base (AFB), California, by Air Materiel Command (AMC) before reassignment to the San Antonio Air Materiel Area at Kelly AFB, Texas, for logistics purposes. This was fairly straightforward, as the C-124 incorporated much commonality with the C-74.

With production deliveries to the USAF completed, the YC-124 no longer had a flying role and was withdrawn from use in October 1957. Soon afterwards, the aircraft was flown to Wright-Patterson AFB, Ohio, and eventually displayed with the Air Force Museum. Sadly, when the museum relocated to its present site, the Globemaster was considered too large to move, and was donated to the station fire department for egress training. Consequently, its useful days were complete, with the aircraft being abandoned, and eventually scrapped.

C-124A

The YC-124 quickly proved to the USAF that the type offered a significant enhancement in capability, as some 90 percent of the Army's weaponry could be airlifted without being dismantled. Furthermore, large vehicles, as well as partly disassembled aircraft and helicopters could be loaded with comparative ease through the clam shell doors.

The USAF was sufficiently impressed with the potential capabilities of such an aircraft, that a single production prototype C-124A, serial 48-0795, was ordered in 1948, followed by 28 operational models a year later. Further orders during 1950 and 1951 eventually amounted to a production run of 204 aircraft.

The production prototype C-124A was retained for 18 months by the manufacturer for assessment, before joining the Military Air Transport Service (MATS). Five Air Transport Squadrons (ATS) at four bases evaluated the aircraft for suitability of their facilities and procedures ahead of these units being allocated their own complement. MATS service began on January 7, 1952, with assignment to the 1291st ATS at Kelly AFB. The squadron was redesignated the 32nd ATS on July 11, 1952, with 48-0795 remaining at Kelly AFB until February 1953 when it was transferred to the 77th ATS at McChord AFB, Washington. However, the aircraft was not completed to full operational specification, and was therefore unable to be assigned to an ATS for conventional missions once the evaluation was complete.

Nevertheless, the requirement to train maintenance technicians with hands-on experience on modern hardware resulted in 48-0795 being flown to Sheppard AFB, Texas, during February 1955 for reassignment to the 3750th Technical Training Group (TTG) as a ground airframe with the designation GC-124A. After years of service, the aircraft was deleted from the inventory and relegated to the dump by April 1964 before being scrapped the following year.

The first three airframes manufactured in the fiscal year (FY) 1949 were devoted to evaluation by Douglas, as well as the principal AMC organizations – which became the Air Research and Development Command on April 2, 1951. Indeed, 49-0232 joined the Wright Air Development Center (WADC) as an EC-124A to conduct an extensive test program, but was destroyed when attempting to make an emergency landing in a field near New Castle, Indiana, on May 23, 1951. Two of the propellers are believed to have reverse pitched, causing the aircraft to lose altitude, before striking a house roof and trees and becoming engulfed in flames.

Undeterred, the other pair continued with the program, to ensure any deficiencies in the aircraft were identified and rectified early. One important function to be evaluated was to certify that the Globemaster was safe to deliver troops into a combat area by parachute. Beginning in November 1952, 49-0233 was flown from Naval Air Station (NAS) El Centro, California, by the 6511th Parachute Development Group in conjunction with the newly formed Air Force Flight Test Center (AFFTC).

Right: **52nd Troop Carrier Squadron (TCS) 51-7284 unloading an Army Sikorsky H-19C Chickasaw at Rhein-Main AB in 1957. (USAF)**

Below: **Wearing MATS titles along the fuselage, the prototype C-124A, 48-0795, was assigned to various bases to be evaluated prior to those facilities receiving their own complement. As the aircraft differed from production models, the airframe was reassigned to Sheppard AFB, Texas, as a ground trainer, which is where this photograph was taken during the mid-1960s.**

Above left: **49-0232 was designated as an EC-124A and served briefly with the Wright Air Development Center (WADC) before being lost in an accident in Indiana on May 23, 1951.**

Above right: **Shortly after roll out at Long Beach in July 1950, EC-124A 49-0233 flew with a variety of evaluation organizations, including the Air Proving Ground at Eglin AFB. (Douglas)**

Interestingly, at least two Globemasters were officially designated as EC-124As for a brief period between 1951 and 1954. Although this would ordinarily indicate that special electronic equipment was installed, in this instance the prefix is believed to signify that the aircraft was exempt from environmental testing for readiness. For some inexplicable reason, the C-124 was exempt from all-weather testing prior to entering service, which resulted in the USAF quickly placing serious restrictions on the aircraft due to icing problems creating a safety hazard. The issue prompted the Flight Test Division at Wright-Patterson AFB to instigate an urgent investigation, which was rectified by Douglas with installation of wing tip combustion heaters for the C-124A model from the 80th airframe onwards. These heaters were retrospectively fitted to some older C-124A models but bizarrely not all.

The first 79 aircraft, up to serial 50-1268, were delivered without wing tip heaters or the weather radar, while the next 85 had the wing tip heaters added. From aircraft 51-0157, both systems were incorporated

Assigned to the WADC, 49-0233 was briefly an EC-124A before reverting to a C-124A, it displays the tail markings and unit emblem of the WADC on the nose. It is at Wright-Patterson AFB in 1956. (Bob Garrard)

A Tactical Air Command (TAC) C-124C being masked prior to being repainted at Greenville, quite possibly during mid-1957 when MATS assumed responsibility for the 130 plus TAC aircraft. (LTV)

during manufacture. Surviving C-124As from 49-0243 onwards were upgraded to C-124C standard, with the installation of wing tip heaters, an APS-42 weather radar housed in a nose-mounted thimble-shaped radome below the cockpit, and slightly more powerful engines. A total of 167 aircraft were modified to full C-124C standard. The first was 50-0112, which was completed on 15 October 1962. Others commenced upgrade soon afterwards, with the majority being converted between March 1963 and March 1965 when the final examples were returned to service. Modifications were undertaken by contractor Hayes Aircraft Corporation of Birmingham, Alabama, but carried out at the home stations of the aircraft, or during major overhaul.

Above left: 51-5182 of the 1502nd Air Transport Wing (ATW) landing at Tachikawa AB, shortly after conversion from a C-124A to a C model on July 3, 1963.

Above right: A 15th TCS C-124 undergoing overhaul at Greenville, Texas, some time prior to July 1957. The yellow docks were wheeled into place to protect the workforce from the intense Texas sun during the summer months. (LTV)

First Deliveries

The majority of the aircraft from the 1949 order were delivered direct to Strategic Air Command (SAC) bases beginning with 49-0235. The aircraft was accepted on July 14, 1950, and delivered three days later, although was not officially taken on charge by the 2nd Strategic Support Squadron at Walker AFB, New Mexico, until the following day. However, 49-0237 was "borrowed" by MATS from SAC for temporary assignment with the 1705th Air Transport Wing (ATW) at McChord AFB during July 1952. The aircraft augmented those of the 1291st and 34th ATSs while the units were in transition.

Despite the C-124 being ideally suited for MATS, it was Tactical Air Command (TAC) that followed SAC in receiving new aircraft. The 62nd Troop Carrier Group (TCG) at McChord AFB accepted delivery of 49-0252 on December 6, 1950. However, to enable MATS to begin conversion to the C-124, SAC relinquished 50-0083 to join the 1274th ATS, a C-97 unit at the time, at Kelly AFB. This aircraft was also flown by various other MATS squadrons for familiarization and training.

Meanwhile, SAC accepted the first 16 of the FY 1950 order, enabling three squadrons to be declared fully operational. Deliveries then switched to TAC with the 7th and 8th TCSs of the 62nd TCG receiving new aircraft at McChord AFB. The Group, along with its aircraft, personnel and equipment, relocated the 200 miles east to Larson AFB, Washington, on April 21, 1952.

MATS deliveries commenced in August 1951 with the 1258th ATS at Brookley AFB, Alabama, receiving its initial complement when 50-0116 was delivered. Other MATS units followed. MATS formed the 1740th ATS on September 5, 1951, as the training unit for C-124 aircrew, firstly at McChord AFB which, from July 1, 1952, relocated to Palm Beach AFB, Florida. The final C-124A was 51-5187, which joined MATS 34th ATS at McChord AFB on February 2, 1953. By this time, the C-124 had participated in the Korean War (1950–53) and had justified the investment that Douglas had in the new design.

The first aircraft to join Strategic Air Command (SAC) was 49-0235, which initiated deliveries in July 1950. SAC C-124 crews had to endure operations to worldwide locations in all weathers. This aircraft is taxiing in snow, possibly at Thule AB, Greenland.

As stated, the majority of A models were eventually upgraded to C-124C standard. Active duty began to relinquish early production aircraft to Continental Air Command (CONAC) for the reserves beginning in April 1961. The remainder continued service with MATS until the middle of the decade when the C-141A entered service in appreciable numbers, and MATS had been replaced by Military Airlift Command (MAC).

Right: C-124A 50-0104 of the 8th TCS, 62nd Troop Carrier Group (TCG), landing at Boise Air Terminal, Idaho, during August 1952. (William T Larkins)

Below: The only unit identification on 51-0120 is the 6th TCS emblem on the nose, seen during the latter stages of the Korea War.

C-124C

Douglas improved the design of the C-124A with the addition of up-rated Pratt & Whitney Wasp engines, offering eight percent more power, as well as wing tip heaters and an APS-42 weather radar. Designated as the C-124C, the first was 51-5188, which joined the Air Force on February 27, 1953. Evaluation by the manufacturer, as well as the San Bernardino Air Materiel Area at Norton AFB, California, and the AFFTC at Edwards AFB preceded assignment to the 62nd Troop Carrier Wing at Larson AFB on July 26, 1954. A total of 243 were constructed before the final example, serial 53-0052, joined the 1501st ATW at Travis AFB, California, on May 6, 1955.

Above: Looking factory-fresh and quite likely shortly after roll-out at Long Beach, 52-1044 gleams in the California sunshine. The aircraft was delivered to the 32nd ATS at McChord AFB on March 29, 1954. (The Aviation Photo Company)

Left: 1501st ATW C-124C 51-0151 unloaded cargo at Royal Australian Air Force East Sale AB, Australia, during 1961. (Kurt Finger)

Below: 61st MAW 51-5202 landing at Hickam AFB. (Nick Williams)

One month after transfer to the 61st MAW at Hickam AFB, 52-1067 is parked at Richmond Airport, Australia, in July 1966. Just visible is the retracted cargo hatch aft of the wing root. (Ben Dannecker)

All the active-duty C-124 units eventually flew the C-124C model, with MATS gradually acquiring the compliments from AMC/Air Force Logistics Command (AFLC), SAC and TAC to become the sole operator of the type for airlift duties. The deactivation of MATS and the change to MAC on January 1, 1966, enabled the USAF, rather than the Department of Defense (DoD), to organize strategic airlift on behalf of the other DoD services. The introduction of the C-141 into MAC service, along with the impending delivery of the C-5A Galaxy permitted the Command to plan for the wholesale retirement of the remaining C-124s or transfer to the reserves. The final examples had departed MAC service by the end of 1969.

YC-124B

Supporting the Korean campaign enabled the C-124 to carve a niche in the airlift world, validating the faith that Douglas designers had in creating the type. While enabling large cargoes to be transported over great distances, the C-124 nevertheless had its drawbacks, most notably the slow pace at which the Globemasters traveled the world. While the commercial airlines were switching to the more capable turboprop and jet designs, the USAF was slow to transition its thinking away from piston-engined aircraft. However, there was a gradual move away from the convention, with Lockheed experimenting with the Allison T56 turboprop engine for the C-130 Hercules, while Douglas was planning the Pratt & Whitney T34 for the C-133 Cargomaster.

Nevertheless, the USAF remained wary and insisted that the new turboprop engines becoming available should be evaluated for possible future programs. Eventually, Douglas, in conjunction with the USAF, announced on December 7, 1950, that a turboprop version of the C-124A was to be developed.

The innovative powerplants offered almost double the horsepower, providing greater speed, higher altitudes, and better fuel efficiency. To enable the USAF to appraise the new technology, MATS activated the 1700th Test Squadron (Turboprop) at Kelly AFB on December 1, 1954, operating two Convair YC-131Cs fitted with the Allison YT56, along with a pair of Boeing YC-97Js, and two Lockheed YC-121F Constellations powered by YT-34s.

Douglas modified 51-0072 with YT-34s, which was a significant improvement over the standard C-124. The YC-124B was pressurized, enabling a service ceiling of 30,000ft (9,154m). A complete pneumatic system was fitted, providing power for starting and to maintain pressurization. The vertical tail was taller and increased in area, and the horizontal stabilizers had a new cross section profile to give better stability and control.

The first flight after conversion was on February 2, 1954, before 51-0072 embarked on a development program, which was carried out primarily by Douglas at Long Beach, and Pratt & Whitney, along with involvement from the AFFTC at Edwards. With sufficient data from two years of trials, the aircraft was withdrawn from use during October 1956. Conceived while the US was engaged in the Korean War, the armistice largely reduced the urgent need for this aircraft. Furthermore, the new C-130 design, with its rough field capability, was more attractive to the USAF than this older adaption.

Due to the radical difference between the YC-124B and standard Globemasters, it was not possible for 51-0072 to perform conventional airlift duties. However, the aircraft gained a second career when flown to the US Army Redstone Arsenal in Huntsville, Alabama, as a grounded munitions-loading trainer. Redstone was associated with all aspects of missile technology. Subsequently, the trainer requirement was completed and the aircraft scrapped.

The aircraft design was also proposed as a tanker version as the KC-124B, although the USAF preferred the KC-97 Stratofreighter, and therefore the Globemaster tanker did not proceed beyond the drawing board.

The YC-124B was not the only dedicated engine development version of the Globemaster. After briefly serving with TAC, 52-1069 was bailed to Pratt & Whitney at Hartford, Connecticut, in December 1954 to be the testbed for the XT-57 axial flow turboprop engine planned for the proposed Douglas C-132. The experimental engine was mounted on the front of the sealed clam shell doors, and was the most powerful turboprop of its kind at the time. However, problems associated with the engine conspired to eventually cancel the project. 52-1069 was initially designated as a JC-124C and from 1957 as an NC-124C. The impending withdrawal of funding for the project, along with the extensive modifications to the aircraft were factors that prevented the aircraft from continuing flying duties, As such, the NC-124C was flown to Davis-Monthan AFB in mid-1958 and placed in storage, where parts were reclaimed as spares for operational Globemasters.

Above: YC-124B 51-0072 seen on static display soon after roll out at Long Beach during 1954. (Douglas)

Left: NC-124C 52-1069 was bailed to Pratt & Whitney at Hartford as a testbed for development of the T57 turboprop engine planned for the proposed Douglas C-132 – an improved version of the C-124, which did not proceed beyond the mock-up stage. (Pratt & Whitney)

Chapter 2

Active Duty Commands and Organizations

The C-124 was operated by more than a dozen different USAF Commands or organizations of similar prominence, with all but one using the type in a flying capacity. For ease of reference, these are listed alphabetically. Note that the dates shown for the unit assignments have been obtained from official records, unless otherwise stated. In these latter circumstances, the dates record when C-124s were being flown by these organizations, and not necessarily when the unit was activated or deactivated. In many instances, the parent Wing was in place before and after the assignment of the C-124, as were several squadrons that were already active, transitioning from other types, such as the C-54. Furthermore many squadrons remained active when exchanging the Globemaster for more modern equipment, such as the C-141 – the dates listed being just for the C-124 period of operations.

Right: 52-0948 served with the 61st MAW for the majority of 1969 before being transferred to the Air Force Reserves (AFRES) and eventually the Tennessee Air National Guard (ANG). (Nick Williams)

Below: 436th MAW C-124C 53-0027 taxiing at Royal Air Force (RAF) Mildenhall during May 1966. Soon afterwards, the aircraft was transferred to the 443rd MAW at Tinker AFB for a brief period, before returning to the 436th to join the Detachment at Rhein-Main AB. (Jeff Peck)

One important aspect that needs explanation is the hierarchical system. During the 1950s and 1960s, C-124s often carried the numerical Group identity on the nose wheel door. Furthermore, the official record cards show individual aircraft delivery to the Group and not the parent Wing. The Wing administered the base, and was responsible for the Group, which in turn, conducted day-to-day operations (similar to the present, whereby the flying activities are organized by the Operations Group, which is subordinate to the parent Wing).

The system of Wings and Groups was in place with the Far East Air Forces, MATS and TAC until the 1960s, while CONAC/Air Force Reserves (AFRES) and the Air National Guard (ANG) retained the Group designations until the 1970s.

Air Materiel Command, Later Air Force Logistics Command

AMC was established on March 9, 1946, to effectively oversee the procurement, maintenance and sustainment of new USAF assets. Air Materiel Areas (AMA) were created geographically to organize and administer the task, frequently in collaboration with the aerospace industry. The C-124 was assigned in small numbers to AMC, with these becoming a vital asset when the Command added responsibility for storage and delivery of nuclear weapons. AMC was redesignated as AFLC on April 1, 1961.

Left: 52-0961 was delivered to the 28th Logistics Support Squadron (LSS) at Hill AFB in December 1953, and was still assigned to the Squadron until April 1969 when retired to MASDC. It was one of the few C-124s to remain with a single unit throughout its entire career.

Below: Air Force Logistics Command (AFLC) C-124s were occasional visitors to the UK SAC bases, as seen here with 19th LSS 52-0971 at RAF Greenham Common during March 1963. (Robin Walker)

C-124 operations were performed by:

Assignment	Squadron	Base	Confirmed Dates
WR AMA	7th LSS	Robins AFB	October 18, 1954, to February 6, 1955
3079th ADW			February 6, 1955, to July 1, 1962
39th LSG			July 1, 1962, to July 1, 1964, then to MATS as 7th ATS (Special) Squadron was due to become the 7th MAS on January 8, 1966, when MATS assets were absorbed into MAC. However, the 7th TCS at McChord AFB was already reserved for this designation, so the 7th ATS became the 58th MAS on January 8, 1966.
SA AMA	19th LSS	Kelly AFB	September 25, 1952, to February 6, 1955
3079th ADW			February 6, 1955, to July 1, 1962
39th LSG			July 1, 1962, to July 1, 1963, to MATS 19th ATS (Special) The squadron flew C-124As until the end of 1960 when the unit upgraded to the C-124C. The unit then joined MATS becoming the 19th ATS (Special) on January 1, 1965, and was absorbed into MAC on January 8, 1966, being redesignated the 19th MAS. Upon transfer to MATS, the parent unit was the 62nd ATW. Despite redesignations and reassignment to different Commands, the squadron remained at Kelly AFB until inactivated on December 22, 1969.
OG AMA	28th LSS	Hill AFB	July 8, 1953, to February 6, 1955
3079th ADW			February 6, 1955, to February 6, 1962 To MATS 28th ATS (Special) Transferred to MATS, becoming the 28th ATS (Special), as part of the 1501st ATW at Travis AFB, CA, but remaining at Hill AFB. Redesignated as the 28th MAS on January 8, 1966. Reassigned to the 62nd MAW on July 8, 1967. The squadron was inactivated on April 8, 1969. Note, the 28th LSS was briefly designated as the 28th Combat Airlift Squadron (CAS) at some time between February 1962 and January 1966.

The first C-124 delivered to AMC was 51-0150, which joined the San Antonio AMA at Kelly AFB on September 12, 1952. Shortly afterwards, the 19th Logistics Support Squadron (LSS) was activated on September 25, 1952, to concentrate on the movement of nuclear weapons and components. The AMC remit was expanded when the task for storage and safeguarding of the USAF's special weapons stockpile was added. The 7th and 28th LSS were formed soon afterwards.

Initially, nuclear weapons activities were administered by the Warner-Robins, Ogden, and San Antonio AMAs at Robins AFB, Hill AFB and Kelly AFB, respectively. However, the increase in the number, variety and location of special weapons highlighted the need for a specialized department that could function expressly for the management of these munitions. The 3079th Aviation Depot Wing (ADW) with headquarters at Wright-Patterson AFB was formed on February 6, 1955, gaining responsibility for the five geographically located existing Aviation Depot Groups/Squadrons situated across the mainland US. These stored weapons and administered support locally for the strategic bomber bases in the vicinity, and were as follows:

3080th ADG/308th ADS at Caribou AFS/Loring AFB, Maine, from December 17, 1951
3081st ADG/3081st ADS at Rushmore AFS/Ellsworth AFB, South Dakota, from February 4, 1952
3082nd ADG/3082nd ADS at Deep Creek AFS/Fairchild AFB, Washington, from April 4, 1952
3083rd ADG/3083rd ADS at Fairfield AFS/Travis AFB, from September 4, 1952
3084th ADG/3084th ADS at Stoney Brook AFS/Westover AFB, Massachusetts, from March 17, 1954.

Other Aviation Depot Squadrons (ADS) were subsequently formed elsewhere in the US close to bases housing aircraft with nuclear weapon capability, as well as one more in the UK and two in Morocco. Furthermore, the 3079th also gained responsibility for the three LSSs and their 36 C-124s.

The Wing and its subordinate units were them transferred to AFLC. The realignment of airlift functions enabled the 3079th ADW and all subordinate units to inactivate on July 1, 1962, with the task of special weapons storage being transferred to Special Weapons Directorate (SWD) and the 39th Logistics Support Group (LSG) at Kelly AFB. The three squadrons eventually joined MATS, with all three gaining

Carrying the emblems of the 19th LSS on the nose, and the 3079th Aviation Depot Wing (ADW) on the tail, 51-0115 was originally delivered to SAC, but was transferred to Air Materiel Command (AMC) on March 30, 1955. (AMC)

ATS (Special) status. Throughout these reassignments, they remained at their prescribed locations as geographically separated units.

In addition to SAC nuclear weapons, the delivery of larger missiles for various other government agencies, such as NASA, was also a responsibility of AMC/AFLC C-124s. Missiles produced at Redstone Arsenal in Alabama were periodically ferried to Cape Canaveral, Florida, or the White Sands missile range in New Mexico.

The centralization of responsibility for the three former LSSs, now MASs, under the 62nd Military Airlift Wing (MAW) enabled the Wing to assume the task of special weapons delivery. The 62nd retained this task when transitioning to the C-141 and with the current Boeing C-17A Globemaster III.

Air Research and Development Command and Air Force Systems Command

Research and Development Command (RDC) was created on January 23, 1950, and was redesignated the Air Research and Development Command (ARDC) on September 16, 1950, then later redesignated as Air Force Systems Command (AFSC) on April 1, 1961. Whereas AMC and AFLC were responsible for the sustainment of assets in service, ARDC and AFSC provided the necessary expertise to evaluate equipment from the period prior to being ordered, through until operational service. In many instances, ARDC/AFSC continued with evaluation long after these assets were in service, to assist with upgrades, improvements, and general developments.

Known C-124 Assignments:

Assignment	Base	Known Dates
WP ARD	Wright-Patterson AFB	June 1951 to February 1954 at least
2750th ABW	Wright-Patterson AFB	February 1953 to September 1954 at least
3200th PTW	Eglin AFB, FL	December 1950 to May 1952 at least
3201nd ABW	Eglin AFB	During September 1963
3200th ABW	Eglin AFB	During September 1953
4901st SW	Kirtland AFB, NM	February 1952 to February 1955 at least
4950th TW	Wright-Patterson AFB	September 1964 to June 1967
6510th ABW	Edwards AFB	November 1952 to June 1954 at least

As previously mentioned, the first C-124, serial 48-0795, was constructed as a prototype, and was not intended for operational service. The aircraft performed company evaluation before being accepted into USAF service, initially by the newly created RDC and later by ARDC. The first three production Globemasters, 49-0232 to 49-0234, also carried out various tests before two eventually joined regular USAF units. These were flown by the WADC, the AFFTC, and the Air Proving Ground at Eglin AFB, Florida. All three organizations were involved in development of new designs to ensure they were capable of effective operational service. Some aircraft were retained by the test centres to continue development work, due to the rapid pace of technology being introduced 49-0233 was still with the WADC in 1956 and later joined CONAC in 1961.

The WADC changed title throughout the 1950s, eventually becoming the Aeronautical Systems Division (ASD) on April 1, 1961, and activating the 4950th Training Wing (TW) on March 1, 1971, to administer all flying activities. Furthermore, the WADC joined the new AFSC. Throughout all the change in titles, the WADC/ASD occasionally borrowed a C-124 from MATS when needed for short-term duties. This included 53-0006 from September 1964, designated as a JC-124C for an unspecified

JC-124C 53-0006 operated by the Aeronautical Systems Division at Wright-Patterson AFB, Ohio, in the summer of 1965. The aircraft was with the development organization from September 1964 to June 1967. (via EMCS)

task, although it is possible the aircraft may have evaluated various upgrades as surviving A models were being converted to C-124C standard. The Globemaster returned to operational service in June 1967, joining the Tennessee ANG, although the designation did not revert to C-124C until October 1967 – more than likely just a delay in making the change, rather than continuing with temporary test duties until this time. NC-124C 52-1069, mentioned earlier, was bailed to Pratt & Whitney by the ARDC, where the aircraft performed engine development between October 1954 and mid 1958. Details are presented at the end of chapter one.

The Air Force Special Weapons Center at Kirtland AFB was responsible for all aspects of nuclear weapons development. As such, the Center was tasked with ensuring nuclear munitions and their components could be transported effectively to operational units. Therefore, C-124 51-0084 was assigned to the 4901st Support Wing at Kirtland AFB in February 1952, and was retained for a number of years to enable evaluation of delivery techniques to be refined. The work of the Center was subsequently incorporated into the operations of the three LSSs. 51-0084 was bailed briefly to North American at Inglewood, California, in February 1953 to the Atomic Energy Research Department, at Inglewood, California a division of North American Aviation involved in nuclear technology including reactors.

Air Training Command

The primary duty of the Air Training Command (ATC) was to educate all personnel in all the trades of the USAF, from their first day joining the military through until graduation, no matter what occupation they would subsequently perform.

After basic and advanced flight training with ATC, new C-124 pilots initially transitioned to the Globemaster through classes organized by their relevant command. Experienced MATS and SAC pilots were given tuition training by Douglas at Long Beach prior to being allocated as instructors within their respective commands. Likewise, qualified and experienced maintenance personnel were also tutored at Long Beach, so they too could instruct personnel at their home stations. SAC initially performed this task, but soon delegated this duty to the "University of MATS."

GC-124A 49-0237 spent the majority of its service life as a ground trainer with the Sheppard Technical Training Center. Duties were varied, but included training personnel with the intricacies of handling Intercontinental Ballistic Missiles (ICBMs.) It is seen during an air show at Sheppard AFB during July 1961.

ATC did not organize flying training squadrons for the C-124, as MATS had established the Heavy Transport Training Unit to perform this function for all of its major aircraft types.

However, technical trades were taught at a host of schools, with the Sheppard Technical Training Center (TTC) at Sheppard AFB, utilizing dozens of surplus airframes to teach the intricacies of aircraft maintenance and repair. In the majority of instances, early examples of new types were invariably made available to the Center as these were either superseded by later models, or were not to the same configuration as operational versions. At least two Globemasters were assigned to this task, designated as GC-124As as they were still officially in the inventory but being used as ground trainers.

48-0795 arrived at Sheppard TTC in March 1955, and continued in residence until April 1964 when it was deleted from the inventory, and eventually scrapped. 49-0237 was formerly stationed at Palm Beach AFB until May 1953, when transferred to Sheppard where it remained until circa 1970. The unit operating the retired airframes was the 3750th Technical Training Squadron, which was part of the similarly numbered Technical Training Wing.

Another C-124A, serial 50-0106, briefly served with MATS until August 28, 1952, when reassigned to Chanute TTC, ATC, at Chanute AFB, Illinois. The C-124 was temporarily with the Flight Engineers School to enable graduates to have "hands-on" experience prior to being reassigned to operational units. The aircraft returned to airlift duties later ahead of joining CONAC.

Alaskan Air Command

As the title suggests, the Alaskan Air Command (AAC) was responsible for the huge land mass comprising the state of Alaska including the host of islands making up the Aleutian chain extending westward across the Bering Strait toward Russia. The AAC was absorbed into the Pacific Air Forces (PACAF) on August 9, 1990.

The AAC borrowed C-124A 51-0100 for assignment to the 39th ADW/5039th Air Base Wing (ABW) at Elmendorf AFB between October 8, 1951, and August 9, 1953. The Globemaster was loaned by the 62nd TCG to enable the Command to evaluate operating procedures ahead of its own aircraft being delivered on October 6, 1952. 51-0159 was the first aircraft to be assigned to the 54th TCS, followed by 12 more that arrived during the following seven weeks. The primary role was that of resupply to smaller military complexes within the state, many of which had no airstrip, thereby preventing the aircraft from landing. Consequently, the C-124 carried out low-level air drops with the aid of parachutes, with cargo ejected through the side doors or dropped from the hatch in the cargo floor. The Squadron flew the C-124 throughout Alaska until July 20, 1956, when the unit was relocated to Donaldson AFB, joining the 63rd TCG. MATS units assumed the tasking from that period onwards.

The withdrawal of dedicated C-124 in 1956 was not the end of the assignment of the type in the state. The Command had C-130s allocated, although some cargo was too bulky to fit into the Hercules, and therefore the task of delivering such items was performed by C-124s of the 62nd MAW from McChord AFB. However, when the 62nd relinquished its C-124s for the C-141A, a pair of 62nd Globemasters joined the 17th TAS, 21st Composite Wing (CW), at Elmendorf in December 1969. One report suggests the C-124s were operated by the 5041st Tactical Operations Squadron from October 1, 1971, although this is unconfirmed.

Six were assigned in total to the AAC, although never more than two at any one time. The AAC was the last organization to operate the C-124, with 51-0075 suffering a ground accident at a small airstrip near Cape Newenham, Alaska, late in September 1972. The fuselage was used as a large boat house until the remains were stuck off charge on October 1, 1974 – thereby officially being the last Globemaster in service. There is a suggestion that following the removal of reusable components, the carcass was blown up!

Parked on the end of a row of C-124s at MASDC, 51-0077 served briefly with the 21st Composite Wing (CW) at Elmendorf AFB until retired on July 11, 1974. One of the few C-124s to enter storage twice, 51-0077 had originally arrived at MASDC on May 26, 1972, but returned to service on 9 February 1973. (Terry Waddington)

AAC C-124s were painted with a large Arctic Red area on the tail, which was similar to the scheme applied to the Globemasters of SAC delivered to the USAF two decades earlier.

C-124 Assignments:

Assignment	Squadron	Base	Confirmed Dates
39th ADW	54th TCS	Elmendorf AFB, Alaska	October 1952 to April 1953
5039th ABW	54th TCS	Elmendorf AFB	April 1953 to June 20, 1956, to Donaldson AFB, SC
21st CW	17th TAS	Elmendorf AFB	December 1969 to October 1, 1974

Note the parent organizations were active as follows: 5039th ADW September 1948 to January 1951; 39th ADW January 1951 to April 1953; 5039th Air Base Wing (ABW) April 1953 to June 1957.

Far East Air Force

The Far East Air Force (FEAF) was established on January 1, 1947, to administer the USAF activities within the western Pacific Ocean area. On July 1, 1957, FEAF was absorbed into the PACAF, amalgamating under a single manager the entire region from the shores of the US West Coast across to South East Asia (SEA).

Right: Shortly after delivery to the 6th TCS at Tachikawa AB, Japan, on May 27, 1952, C-124A 51-0114 joined the Far East Air Force (FEAF), but remained largely anonymous while supporting the Korean War.

Below: Initially delivered to the 374th TCW at Tachikawa AB in June 1952, 51-0121 had its serial presented as 1121. No unit insignia or identity is carried, although the 6th TCS badge was applied to the nose later. (FEAF)

FEAF C-124 Assignments:

Assignment	Squadron	Base	Confirmed Dates
FEAF HQ	4th TCS	Tachikawa AB, JP	September 24, 1951, to November 16, 1951
		Tachikawa AB	Operations from November 16, 1951, to January 22, 1952, administered by FEAF HQ. Assets returned to Air Proving Ground.
	374th TCW	Tachikawa AB	
	374th TCG	Tachikawa AB	October 15, 1946, to November 18, 1958
	6th TCS	Tachikawa AB	May 1952 to November 18, 1958
	22nd TCS	Tachikawa AB	May 1952 to July 1, 1957

The C-124 started to be delivered to the USAF just four weeks after North Korea launched its invasion of the South on June 25, 1950. The United Nations responded quickly to the situation, with a coalition of allies supporting the resolution to defend the South. Initially, C-47s, C-54s and Fairchild C-119 Boxcars were the USAF mainstay of the airlift requirement, although there was clearly a need for a trial within the combat zone for an aircraft with an increased capacity such as the C-124. The FEAF – forerunner of today's PACAF in the region – was anxious to utilize the C-124 to support combat operations. On September 24, 1951, Air Proving Ground C-124A 49-0256 was flown to Tachikawa Air Base (AB), Japan, for duty with the 4th TCS to enable the FEAF to conduct service tests under operational conditions. The aircraft flew 26 missions between Japan and Korea in less than 40 days, carrying an average load of 34,000lb (15.4 tonnes), which was double the capacity of the C-54. In one mission, a C-124 airlifted a record 167 patients from Pusan East AB, South Korea, to Japan. The tests were successfully completed, enabling the C-124 to return to Eglin AFB on January 22, 1952.

Having proved the C-124 was an ideal asset for the campaign, the FEAF was anxious to add the Globemaster to its inventory. The first C-124A, serial 51-0111, arrived in the Far East on May 25, 1952, joining the 374th TCW at Tachikawa AB. The aircraft flew its first operational FEAF mission on July 3, 1952. A further 12 C-124s were delivered new to the Wing for combat operations within four weeks. A dozen more were assigned, commencing on August 7, 1952. Missions were primarily delivering troops and equipment to the combat zone, and repatriating wounded personnel to Japan. TAC C-124s were utilized to transport patients across the Pacific Ocean to hospitals in the US. By the time of the armistice in June 1953, the C-124 had validated its combat effectiveness.

A fine view of 1503rd ATW C-124A 51-0142 visiting Darwin, Australia, during 1958. Note the larger-than-usual white area applied to the upper forward fuselage, which would appear to be specific to aircraft stationed in the Pacific region. (Airhistory.net)

51-0120 of the 1503rd ATW departing Tachikawa AB during November 1961.

The end of the war enabled the FEAF C-124s to begin peacetime airlift operations within the region. However, as part of the reorganization of strategic airlift assets worldwide, the 374th TCW inactivated on July 1, 1957, with the C-124s transferred to the 1503rd ATW, which formed on July 15, 1957, under MATS to conduct operations within the region. The 22nd TCS was non-operational from July 1, 1957, until February 1959. The MATS/MAC C-124 units located at Tachikawa flew across the western Pacific Ocean area until inactivated on June 8, 1969. (See more in the Pacific Air Forces section).

Military Air Transport Service and Military Airlift Command

MATS was formed on June 1, 1948, to provide a joint operator of the Army Air Forces Air Transport Service with that of certain US Navy's transport squadrons. The Service was part of the new USAF, but was controlled directly by the DoD. MATS was a "Unified Command," established to serve the military with operating units combined jointly from more than one DoD component under a single manager. However, the DoD administration of MATS was not ideal, primarily as the USAF was not in total control. Furthermore, MATS was not a Major Command, despite operating at the same level as its contemporaries. Therefore, on January 1, 1966, MATS was replaced by MAC, affording the USAF direct control of all activities.

As explained at the beginning of the chapter, the structure of MATS was somewhat confusing, as the parent numbered Wing was in place alongside a similarly numbered group. Furthermore, there was more than one group assigned or attached! For example, the 63rd TCW was originally activated as a TAC unit on January 8, 1953, until transferred to MATS in its entirety on July 1, 1957. The 61st ATG was attached between August 25, 1954 and June 30, 1957, and assigned between July 1, 1957 and October 8, 1959. Furthermore, the 63rd ATG was a component of the parent Wing between June 20, 1953, and January 18, 1963. To confuse the situation even more, the 64th TCG was attached between October 15, 1953, and February 15, 1954, but was not a C-124 unit. A similar situation was in place for the 62nd ATW, which was activated on September 17, 1951, with the 61st ATG attached November 21, 1952, to August 24, 1954, and the 62nd ATG between October 1, 1951, and January 15, 1960. Groups assigned were directly operated, while those attached were for operational control during a limited period. If that was not perplexing enough, there were periods when the Wing was inactive, with only Groups in place. Refer to the unit tabulation for the details.

Above: C-124C 51-7276 at Alconbury in May 1959, wearing the Arctic Red tail color scheme. The design was being phased out at the time, as aircraft received major overhaul and repaint.

Left: 63rd TCW 52-0955 exhibited at Sculthorpe during May 1962. Rhein-Main's rotational C-124s were frequent participants at European air shows. (via EMCS)

Below: After spending many years with the 63rd TCW/MAW and being regularly detached to Rhein-Main AB, 51-5205 was transferred to the 61st MAW at Hickam AFB in May 1969. However, six months later, the aircraft relocated to the AFRES. (Nick Williams)

Upon transfer to MATS, the former TAC units retained their designation identities until MAC was formed, when they all changed to MAS/Ws. Although the Group system was eliminated for the larger units, the 65th remained as a MAG due to being a smaller unit and not operating aircraft directly assigned, instead flying C-124s detached from elsewhere.

MATS' own units were similarly organized. The 1501st ATW at Fairfield-Suisun AFB (renamed Travis AFB from October 20, 1950) was activated on July 1, 1955. However, the 1501st ATG was formed on May 16, 1953, as the primary unit to administer operations until the parent wing was formed. The group was in place until inactivated on 18 January 1963.

52-0944 of the 1501st ATW at Travis AFB. The Day-Glo orange was a feature until 1963 when the bright color had been removed.

51-5198 of the 60th MAW in Australia at Richmond AB during February 1967. The Globemaster was damaged at Hickam AFB on March 6, 1968, and following cannibalization, was SOC almost a year later. (Ben Dannecker)

Assignment	Squadron	Base	Confirmed Dates
60th MAW		Travis AFB	January 8, 1966, to November 1991* (ex-1501st ATW)
	28th MAS	Hill AFB	January 8, 1966, to July 8, 1967
	85th MAS	Travis AFB	January 8, 1966, to July 8, 1967

61st MAW C-124C 53-0038 departing the home station during February 1968. The aircraft was retired in April 1969 without having performed any reservist service. (Nick Williams)

Australia was occasionally a destination for 61st MAW C-124s 51-5180 is at Richmond, New South Wales, in July 1966. Various US government operations in the country required resupply with C-124s. (Ben Dannecker)

Assignment	Squadron	Base	Confirmed Dates
61st MAW		Hickam AFB	January 8, 1966, to December 22, 1969 (ex-1502nd ATW)
	6th MAS		January 8, 1966, to June 8, 1968
	50th MAS		January 8, 1966, to December 22, 1969

53-0009 served the 1607th ATW and 436th MAW from delivery in October 1954 until March 1966, when it was transferred to the 61st MAW at Hickam AFB. It is seen at Richmond Airport in May 1966. (Ben Dannecker)

C-124A 50-0112 of the 62nd TCW visiting Cedar Rapids, Iowa. (Clyde Gerdes)

Assignment	Squadron	Base	Confirmed Dates
	62nd TCW	Larson AFB	July 1, 1957, to June 13, 1960
		McChord AFB	June 13, 1960, to January 8, 1966
	62nd TCG		July 1, 1957, to January 15, 1960
62nd MAW		McChord AFB	January 8, 1966, to December 1, 1991*
	4th TCS		July 1, 1957, to July 8, 1962
	4th ATS		July 8, 1962, to January 8, 1966
	4th MAS		January 8, 1966, to August 1966
	7th TCS		July 1, 1957, to January 8, 1966
	7th MAS		January 8, 1966, to December 22, 1969
	8th TCS		July 1, 1957, to January 1, 1965
	8th ATS		January 1, 1965, to January 8, 1966
	8th MAS		January 8, 1966, to August 1966
	19th ATS	Kelly AFB	January 1, 1965, to January 8, 1966
	19th MAS	Kelly AFB	January 8, 1966, to December 22, 1969
	28th MAS	Hill AFB	July 8, 1967, to April 8, 1969

Basking in unusually good weather, 62nd ATW C-124 50-1258 at Shemya AFB, Alaska, during 1964.

Assignment	Squadron	Base	Confirmed Dates
63rd TCW		Donaldson AFB	July 1, 1957, to April 1, 1963
		Hunter AFB	April 1, 1963, to January 8, 1966
	61st TCG		July 1, 1957, to October 8, 1959
	63rd TCG		July 1, 1957, to January 18, 1963
63rd MAW		Hunter AFB	January 8, 1966, to April, 1, 1967 (to Norton AFB)
	7th ATS	Robins AFB	July 1, 1964, to January 8, 1966, redesignated as 58th MAS on 8 January 1966
	3rd TCS		July 1, 1957, to December 8, 1960
	9th TCS		July 1, 1957, to January 18, 1963
	14th TCS		July 1, 1957, to January 8, 1966
	14th MAS		January 8, 1966, to April 1, 1967
	15th TCS		July 1, 1957, to January 8, 1966
	15th MAS		January 8, 1966, to March 31, 1967
	52nd TCS		July 1, 1957, to January 8, 1966, with 1602nd ATG at Rhein-Main AB
	52nd MAS		January 8, 1966, to January 8, 1967
	53rd TCS		July 1, 1957, to January 8, 1966
	53rd MAS		January 8, 1966, to July 8, 1966

Another variation of the nose markings applied to TAC aircraft – this version showing the 53rd TCS markings on 51-5186.

Assignment	Squadron	Base	Confirmed Dates
	54th TCS		July 1, 1957, to June 25, 1965
	58th MAS	Robins AFB	January 1, 1966, to July 1, 1966
	65th MAG	Tachikawa AB	January 8, 1966, to June 8, 1969
	22nd MAS		January 8, 1966, to June 8, 1969

Note: Operated aircraft detached from the 61st MAW at Hickam, as well as others from the 63rd MAW at Hunter.

Apart from detaching aircraft on a regular basis to Rhein-Main AB, the 63rd TCW/MAW also periodically deployed C-124s to Tachikawa, as seen here with 51-5190. These were operated by the 65th MAG while in the Pacific theater, but remained assigned to the 63rd.

436th MAW C-124C 51-7279 at Lakenheath, UK, in May 1968.

Assignment	Squadron	Base	Confirmed Dates
	436th MAW	Dover AFB, DE	January 8, 1966, to December 1, 1991* (ex-1607th ATW)
	9th MAS		January 8, 1966, to January 1966
	31st MAS		January 8, 1966, to April 4, 1969
	52nd MAS	Rhein-Main AB, West Germany	January 8, 1967, to February 8, 1969
	58th MAS	Robins AFB	July 1, 1966, to January 8, 1967

436th MAW 52-0950 with the hydraulic ramps extended to unload cargo at Alconbury, UK, in June 1968. (Lindsay Peacock)

436th MAW C-124C 53-0008 rolling to the end of the runway at Mildenhall during May 1968. Note the three USAF C-47s parked outside the hanger. (Jeff Peck)

Assignment	Squadron	Base	Confirmed Dates
	437th MAW	Charleston AFB, SC	January 8, 1966, to October 1, 1991* (ex-1608th ATW)
	17th MAS		January 8, 1966, to April 8, 1969

52-1064 of the 437th MAW showing a fairly clean underside during departure from Hickam AFB during late 1968. (Nick Williams)

443rd MAW C-124C 53-0031 in early 1967 overflying Oklahoma during a training flight. The 443rd did not usually apply any insignia to its C-124s, as assignment to the unit was relatively short. (via Gary Baker)

Assignment	Squadron	Base	Confirmed Dates
	443rd MAW	Tinker AFB, OK	January 8, 1966, to August 27, 1991* (ex-1707th ATW)
	56th MAS		January 8, 1966, to December 1968
	1501st ATW	Travis AFB	July 1, 1955, to January 8, 1966
	1501st ATG		May 16, 1953, to January 18, 1963
	28th ATS	Hill AFB	July 1, 1964, to January 8, 1966
	75th ATS		April 1960 to November 1965
	77th ATS		November 20, 1953, to July 1, 1955
	84th ATS		May 16, 1953, to September 1959
	85th ATS		May 16, 1953, to January 8, 1966
	1502nd ATW	Hickam AFB	July 1, 1955, to January 8, 1966 (1501st ATG prior)
	1500th ATG		October 1, 1948, to May 15, 1958
	1502nd ATG		July 1, 1955, to May 15, 1958
	1503rd ATG		June 22, 1964, to January 8, 1966, at Tachikawa
	6th TCS		June 22, 1964, to January 8, 1966
	48th ATS		July 20, 1952, to March 25, 1965
	50th ATS		July 20, 1952, to January 8, 1966
	51st ATS		July 20, 1952, to July 1, 1955

Displaying the emblem of the 50th ATS on the tail, C-124C 51-0102 flies over the Pacific Ocean while on a paratrooping sortie from Hickam AFB. (USAF)

Assignment	Squadron	Base	Confirmed Dates
	1503rd ATW	Tachikawa AB	November 18, 1958, to June 22, 1964
	1503rd ATG	Tachikawa AB	July 15, 1953, to January 8, 1966
	6th TCS		November 18, 1958, to June 22, 1964
	22nd TCS		November 18, 1958, to January 8, 1966

C-124Cs 51-0129 and 51-0102 both of the 50th ATS, 1502nd ATW, from Hickam AFB in formation to conduct parachute training during 1964. (USAF)

51-0112 of the 1503rd ATW on static display at Wellington, New Zealand, during November 1959. (Ray Massey)

Assignment	Squadron	Base	Confirmed Dates
	1600th ATW	Westover AFB	October 1, 1948, to July 1, 1953 (to 1600th ABW July 1, 1953, to April 1, 1955)
	1600th ATG		October 1, 1948, to June 19, 1955
	15th ATS		July 20, 1952, to April 20, 1955
	20th ATS		July 20, 1952, to May 20, 1955
	31st ATS		July 20, 1952, to May 9, 1955
	1251st ATS		by May 1952 to July 20, 1952, to 15th ATS
	1258th ATS		during October 1951 to July 20, 1952, to 31st ATS

Right: C-124C 53-0045 of the 1607th ATW unloading a Thor missile in the East of England. Under Project *Emily*, the US deployed 60 missiles to 20 RAF bases in the UK, although their period of assignment was relatively short. The first arrived in August 1958 and they were removed within five years.

Below: Six 1607th ATW C-124Cs on the main ramp at Dover AFB, circa 1960. The lead aircraft is 52-1037.

Assignment	Squadron	Base	Confirmed Dates
	1607th ATW	Dover AFB	January 1, 1954, to January 8, 1966
	1607th ATG		January 1, 1954, to January 18, 1963
	1st ATS		September 9, 1954, to May 7, 1960
	9th TCS		January 1, 1965, to January 8, 1966
	15th ATS		April 20, 1955, to January 1, 1965
	20th ATS		May 20, 1955, to January 1, 1965
	20th TCS		January 1, 1965, to July 1, 1965
	21st ATS		November 18, 1953, to July 1, 1955
	31st ATS		July 1, 1955, to June 1, 1965
	31st TCS		June 1, 1965, to January 8, 1966
	40th ATS		May 1, 1954, to December 1960
	45th ATS		February 16, 1954, to July 1, 1955
	1608th ATW	Charleston AFB	March 1, 1955, to January 8, 1966
	1608th ATG		July 1, 1955, to January 8, 1966
	3rd ATS		June 18, 1958, to August 1965
	17th ATS		July 18, 1954, to January 8, 1966
	1700th ATW	Kelly AFB	June 1, 1948, to December 18, 1957
	1700th ATG		October 1, 1948, to December 18, 1957
	3rd ATS		June 18, 1957, to November 24, 1957

Although carrying no unit identification, 52-1042 served with the 1608th ATW at Charleston AFB during the early 1960s, and was still stationed there when the Wing was redesignated as the 437th MAW.

Assignment	Squadron	Base	Confirmed Dates
	76th ATS		July 20, 1952, to February 1, 1956, ex-1291st ATS
	1262nd ATS		circa early 1952 to July 20, 1952
	1274th ATS		during November 1951 to August 1, 1952
	1280th ATS		October 24, 1951 to March 7, 1952
	1289th ATS		March 7, 1952 to July 20, 1952
	1291st ATS		July 24, 1951, to March 7, 1952
	1703rd ATW	Brookley AFB	October 1948 to June 18, 1957
	1703rd ATG		October 25, 1949, to June 18, 1957
	3rd ATS		July 20, 1952, to June 18, 1957
	1258th ATS		August 1951 to July 20, 1952
	1705th ATW	McChord AFB	August 24, 1950, to June 18, 1960
	1705th ATG		August 1, 1950, to June 18, 1960
	32nd ATS		July 20, 1952, to June 18, 1960
	34th ATS		July 20, 1952, to July 1, 1955
	77th ATS		September 24, 1952, to November 19, 1953
	1280th ATS		March 7, 1952, to July 20, 1952
	1289th ATS		January 24, 1952, to March 7, 1952
	1291st ATS		March 7, 1952, to July 20, 1952
	1740th ATS		September 5, 1951, to July 1, 1952

52-0945 of MATS Continental Division assigned to the 3rd ATS, 1703rd ATW, at Brookley AFB transiting Lajes AB, Azores, during 1956. (Paul Zogg collection)

Assignment	Squadron	Base	Confirmed Dates
	1707th ATW	Palm Beach AFB	July 1, 1952, to July 1, 1959
		Tinker AFB	June 1, 1959, to June 8, 1966
	1707th ATG		September 21, 1951, to September 1, 1953
	1740th ATS		July 1, 1952, to January 8, 1966
	1240th ATS	Palm Beach	October 1952 to unknown (at least Nov 1953)

Note that the * indicates the unit changed title, rather than being inactivated – these having the word Military deleted from the Military Airlift Wing designation.

52-1003 began life with the 1740th ATS at Palm Beach AFB in the training role, before joining the 1607th ATW at Dover AFB. It is seen here at Meacham Field, Fort Worth, Texas, during June 1958.

52-1003 after having changed the Arctic Red for Day-Glo orange, circa 1960.

While the ARDC was carrying out test and evaluation, the MATS was experimenting with C-124s flying operational missions. The 1703rd ATG/W at Brookley AFB performed these route-proving flights, initially with the 1258th ATS (later 3rd ATS). 1703rd C-124s flew to the main cargo hubs including Travis AFB and Dover AFB to load cargo for their destinations to ensure the evaluation was realistic. The initial assignment for the 1258th was 50-0116, 50-0117 and 50-0118, which all joined the squadron on October 8, 1951, after a brief period with TAC.

The MATS moved from Brookley AFB on June 18, 1957, when the 1703rd was inactivated. By this time, route proving was complete, with the C-124 established as the primary freighter for all global missions. C-124s quickly established a network of schedules to various worldwide military locations. These were similar to a timetable and commenced from one of MATS' seaboard bases, fanning out to deliver cargo, mail and passengers to various gateway air bases such as Burtonwood and Mildenhall UK; Chateauroux, France; Rhein-Main, West Germany; Incirlik, Turkey; and Torrejon, Spain. Across the Pacific Ocean, MATS island hopped to Hickam, Hawaii; Anderson, Guam; Wake Island; Clark, Philippines; and various Japanese and South Korean destinations. In addition, a host of ad hoc sorties were arranged to support the movement of tactical fighter and strategic bomber deployments overseas. MATS also responded to humanitarian emergencies, usually involving an unexpected and urgent reshuffling of sorties to free up aircraft to fly aid to the particular area in need.

An ad hoc mission with a difference. Following the accident involving a Trans-Canada Air Lines DC-8, which over ran the runway on November 6, 1963, 1607th ATW C-124C 52-1033 brought replacement engines and other components to Heathrow Airport to enable repairs to be carried out. (Brian Stainer)

Supporting the United Nations (UN) in Africa required almost all aid to be airlifted, including vehicles. A white UN truck is unloaded from 53-0046 circa 1961.

From the earlier C-124 period, all MATS' Groups and Wings were designated with four-digit identities within the range 1500, 1600 and 1700. Likewise, the majority of ATSs were numbered with four digits within the range 1200 and 1700. However, many of these were replaced beginning in 1952 by those with one- and two-digit identities. The transfer of the 62nd and 63rd TAC Wings in 1957, along with their TCSs, retained their TAC designations until the 1960s. However, most were redesignated when MATS was replaced by MAC in January 1966.

Apart from being stationed at bases across the US, MATS also had aircraft located in Hawaii and Japan. Initially, units were formed into the Atlantic, Pacific and Continental Divisions, activated in June 1948, with title approximated to their area of responsibility. However, there was a certain ambiguity attached to the regions within which they operated, with a degree of overlap.

Above: Featuring mixed command markings, 51-0167 appears to display the 53rd TCS emblem on the nose as well 63rd TCW stylized nose markings from the period of TAC service, but has been reassigned to MATS Continental Division. This would date the image to the second half of 1957.

Left: A very evocative image of four C-124s all decorated with the Arctic scheme, which was only applied for a short while. 51-0179 is displaying "Continental Division" within the tail band, while 51-0158 is from the Pacific Division. The image is possibly from February 1954, when the former was transferred to the 48th ATS at Hickam AFB.

MATS Atlantic Division	Westover AFB	June 1948 to May 1955
	McGuire AFB	June 1955 to June 1958
Retitled to Eastern Transport Air Force at McGuire AFB July 1958 until inactivated in January 1966		
MATS Continental Division	Kelly AFB	June 1948 to June 1958
Transferred into Western Transport Air Force at Travis AFB, July 1958, until inactivated in January 1966		
MATS Pacific Division	Hickam AFB	June 1948 to June 1958
Retitled to Western Transport Air Force, also at Travis AFB, July 1958, until inactivated in January 1966		

The Atlantic Division was located at Westover AFB and later McGuire AFB, providing regular and unscheduled services across the Atlantic Ocean to Europe, the Caribbean and South America, North Africa and the Middle East as far as Dhahran, Saudi Arabia.

The Pacific Division at Travis AFB was responsible for services to Hawaii and all locations across the Pacific Ocean. This included Japan and the Philippines, SEA, India, Pakistan and Dhahran, Saudi Arabia.

The Continental Division at Kelly AFB had jurisdiction for the US and Canada, along the North Atlantic coast to Thule AB, Greenland. On the western side of the US, jurisdiction included Travis AFB north to McChord AFB and onward to Alaska and Aleutian Islands, including Shemya AFB. A connection was also established to Tachikawa AB, Japan. Within the continental United States, the Division provided coast-to-coast aeromedical evacuation flights as well as cargo services between the major USAF AMC depots. The replacement of the Divisions with the Eastern and Western Transport Air Forces was the precursor to the numbered Air Forces introduced later, and the change helped to streamline operations geographically.

MATS had been called upon to respond to world crises since the day the Service was formed, most with little or no advanced warning. For example, in June 1960, the Belgian Congo became independent, and

MATS Pacific Division C-124 51-0133 unloading cargo in Japan during 1955.

almost immediately became embroiled in a civil war. The United Nations organized troops to be flown in from many nations to restore order. MATS was the primary airlift source, with the C-124 performing the lion's share. Missions were often hazardous, in particular on December 7, 1961, when 51-5208 took 42 hits from small arms fire while landing at Leopoldville Republic of the Congo. Some punctured wing fuel tanks, but miraculously none caused a fire. After emergency repairs were carried out, the aircraft was flown to Châteauroux France, for more effective restoration.

The construction of the Berlin Wall in 1961 raised the level of tension between NATO and the Warsaw Pact countries significantly, as did the 1962 Cuban Missile Crisis. To evaluate the movement of an entire

C-124C 51-7279 at Donaldson AFB during 1958, with the 3rd TCS emblem on the fin, shortly before the Continental Division was replaced by the Western Transport Air Force. (63rd TCW Association)

Left: **63rd MAW C-124C 51-5208 at Mildenhall early in 1966. On December 7, 1961, this aircraft took 42 hits from small arms fire while landing at Leopoldville, Republic of the Congo, supporting Operation** *New Tape*.

Below: **Performing an early period sortie to Tan Son Nhut AB, South Vietnam, during April 1964, 62nd TCW C-124 50-0103 taxis to a parking apron. (Nick Williams)**

Division of 15,500 troops and their personal equipment, the USAF organized Exercise *Big Lift* in October 1963 – see Chapter 4.

As stated, MATS took over control of the C-124s of TAC on July 1, 1957, acquiring some 130 aircraft, and had acquired those of SAC by 1961, adding a further 48. Additionally, AMC/AFLC C-124s also joined MATS around the same time, resulting in the Service being assigned virtually every operational Globie. By 1963, there were 394 C-124s in active duty, with 377 assigned to MATS operated by seven Wings and one Group, composed into 23 Squadrons.

The transfer of TAC aircraft initially placed the 62nd and 63rd TCWs under the Continental Division along with responsibility for Donaldson and Larson AFBs. Between them, the two TCWs were responsible for ten TCSs, some of which were later reassigned between the Divisions to equalize the workload.

The situation remained largely unchanged until January 1, 1966, when MAC was formed. Thereafter, MAC transferred more and more C-124s to the reserves each year until 1969 when the last examples had relocated.

Above left: **Five months after MATS changed to Military Air Command (MAC), C-124C 52-0955 of the 63rd MAW taxis to the end of the runway at Tempelhof Airport, Berlin, during May 1966. (Ralf Manteufel)**

Above right: **C-124 sorties ranged far and wide, with 61st MAW 51-7275 seen landing at Taipei Airport, Taiwan, in January 1969. (Steve Miller)**

Below: **The 61st MAW flew to destinations across the vast Pacific Ocean region, island hopping throughout the area to deliver a wide range of cargo. 52-1083 is at a South East Asian air base during mid-1969. (via EMCS)**

Above: A bulldozer being unloaded from C-124 52-1038 in South Vietnam. Within C-124 community folklore is a tale about a giant bulldozer that was shuffled about Europe and North Africa as training cargo. The 'dozer was transported to a base in West Germany and unloaded, where it remained until the next C-124 crew had to relocate the machine to a base in Libya, and so on for many weeks.

Left: 53-0004 of 61st MAW on a resupply flight in Australia in March 1967. (Ben Dannecker)

On January 1, 1969, MAC had the following 135 C-124s assigned:

Wing	Squadron	Base	Number of C-124s
61st MAW	50th MAS	Hickam AFB	20 aircraft
	22nd MAS	Tachikawa AB	14 aircraft
62nd MAW	7th MAS	McChord AFB	19 aircraft
	19th MAS	Kelly AFB	18 aircraft
	28th MAS	Hill AFB	16 aircraft
436th MAW	31st MAS	Dover AFB	15 aircraft
	52nd MAS	Rhein-Main AB	17 aircraft
437th MAW	17th MAS	Charleston AFB	16 aircraft

Above left: **A rare image of 61st MAW 52-1011 at Hickam AFB in May 1969, in the process of being transferred from MAC to the 937th Military Airlift Group (MAG) at Tinker AFB. The 61st had removed all insignia ahead of the aircraft departing. (Nick Williams)**

Above right: **A tranquil Pacific Islands location for 61st MAW 51-5190, seen taxiing during 1968. Trans-Pacific sorties often involved island-hopping to refuel, crew rest, or to repair engine faults.**

MATS University

The 1740th ATS (Training) was activated on September 5, 1951, at McChord AFB, training aircrew and maintenance personnel on all MATS heavy airlifters, including the Boeing C-54, C-97 Stratofreighter, Douglas C-118 Liftmaster, and the C-124. The first C-124s delivered to MATS for training were 50-1256, 50-1257, 50-1258, and 50-1259, which all joined the 1740th ATS on September 17, 1951. The unit, which was known as the "MATS University," relocated to Palm Beach AFB in July 1952. However, the number of localized training sorties was more than the region could safely handle. Private flying and airline traffic in the area was expanding greatly at this time, and this, coupled with urban development in Florida, forced the relocation of the Wing to Tinker AFB on June 1, 1959. Again, the development of Tinker AFB for other tasks coincided with the formation of MAC January 1, 1966, resulting in the

During the first three years of the 1960s, the UN responded to the crisis in the former Belgian Congo with numerous resupply flights to the country as well as neighbouring nations. Under Operation *New Tape*, MATS flew 2,300 sorties to the region. Here, C-124 52-0945 unloads at Kinshasa's Kamina Airport Republic of the Congo, in May 1962.

1707th ATW inactivating. In its place, MAC on activated the 443rd MAW at Altus AFB, Oklahoma, as the primary airlift training center. Altus was ideal, as its remote setting enabled localized flying and take-off and landing training to proceed within a secluded area.

Pacific Air Force

Pacific Air Force was formed on July 1, 1954, to administer the majority of the activities taking place within the area of the Ocean of the same name. Pacific Air Force was a component of FEAF until July 1, 1957, when the two organizations were amalgamated to become PACAF. No C-124s were directly assigned until February 1970.

Assignment	Squadron	Base	Confirmed Dates
463rd TAW	20th OS	Clark AB	February 1970 to November 1971

PACAF strategic airlift was performed by MATS and MAC until it withdrew C-124s from the 61st MAW at Hickam AFB at the end of December 1969. To redress this resource, four C-124Cs, 52-1073, 52-1078, 52-1082, and 51-1086 were acquired to join 20th Operations Squadron (OS), 463rd TAW at Clark AB. They began arriving on February 12, 1970. They were briefly placed in storage and administered by the 6200th ABW before commencing flying duties. 52-1073 was replaced by 52-1031 and returned to the US while the others continued the tasking, although this was short-lived as the four returned to the US during November 1971 when the type was being retired. Three were retired, while the fourth returned to ANG service.

Throughout their brief period of PACAF assignment, the markings of their previous operators were painted out and the aircraft flown anonymously. Their duties were primarily to deliver outsized loads within the western Pacific region.

Strategic Air Command

SAC was already in place when the USAF was separated from the Army in 1947. It was the iron fist of retaliation, equipped with strategic bombers and aerial-refueling tankers. Legendary commander General Curtis LeMay was adamant that his command would be as self-sufficient as possible, even to the extent of having its own transport capability.

Above left: 2nd Strategic Support Squadron (SSS) C-124A 49-0241 at Detroit air show in September 1952. The colorful patterns on SAC C-124s were relatively short lived, as all too quickly the aircraft were painted with a similar scheme to MATS Globemasters, with the Milky Way fuselage sash to distinguish them. (Bob Pauley)

Above right: SAC C-124A 49-0249, seen at Selfridge AFB, Michigan, during July 1951, was unusual as it was devoid of markings.

SAC C-124 assignments:

Assignment	Squadron	Base	Confirmed Dates
Nil	1st SSS*	Biggs AFB, TX	January 21, 1951, to January 1, 1959
Nil	2nd SSS*	Walker AFB	July 18, 1950, to May 16, 1951
		Castle AFB, CA	May 16, 1951, to September 1, 1956
		Pinecastle AFB, FL	September 1, 1956, to May 7, 1958
		McCoy AFB, FL	May 7, 1958, to June 3, 1961
Nil	3rd SSS	Hunter AFB	December 14, 1950, to January 5, 1953
		Barksdale AFB, LA	January 5, 1953, to June 5, 1961
Nil	4th SSS	Ellsworth AFB	August 14, 1953, to June 15, 1957
		Dyess AFB, TX	June 15, 1957, to February 10, 1961
3902nd ABW	Nil	Offutt AFB	May 1952 and May 1953

* Indicates equipped with the C-54 or C-97 prior to the C-124 being delivered.

When Gen LeMay became the boss of SAC on October 19, 1948, he was alarmed to discover that strategic bombers such as the Convair B-36 Peacemaker were being used to ferry nuclear weapons between bases, instead of being maintained on readiness to retaliate against the Soviet Union. LeMay telephoned his long-time friend Col Avery "Jack" Ladd and instructed him go to Long Beach, California, and "buy me some transport planes to carry my nukes." Donald Douglas showed Col Ladd the C-124 program, and he viewed the production facility where the first example was being constructed. Ladd was so impressed that he reported back to LeMay that the Globemaster was indeed ideal for the "special weapons support." In his well-known uncompromising manner, LeMay ordered the initial production of the C-124 to be delivered to SAC, even ahead of MATS, which had instigated the requirement!

As the first aircraft emerged from Long Beach, Col Ladd was placed in charge of organizing its introduction into service. While the initial three examples were retained by the manufacturer and various test establishments, 49-0235 was the first to join the USAF, and was collected personally by Col Ladd and flown to Walker AFB to join the 2nd Strategic Support Squadron (SSS). The aircraft was officially delivered on July 18, 1950. Having established the initial Squadron, Col Ladd next instituted the C-124 with the 1st SSS at Biggs AFB on January 21, 1951. Col Ladd was then placed in control of both, as well as the 3rd SSS at Hunter AFB and the 4th SSS at Rapid City AFB (later Ellsworth AFB), formed on February 16, 1950, and February 18, 1953, respectively – these being activated some months before receiving their first C-124s.

SAC eventually operated 39 C-124As, and 21 C-124Cs, with the vast majority serving until the summer of 1961, when the Command's transportation tasks and aircraft were transferred to MATS. Throughout the dozen years of operations, the two primary roles were to ferry special weapons between bases worldwide, and the Aviation Depot Groups where AMC stored and maintained these weapons – see AMC section earlier. The other task was to provide the invaluable transportation of personnel and equipment to SAC deployment bases around the world. However, with insufficient aircraft to complete these roles completely "in house," SAC frequently called upon MATS for assistance.

The three LSSs, detailed under AMC earlier, also worked closely alongside SAC, to transport special weapons worldwide using C-124s. The 7th, 19th and 28th LSSs specialized in the delivery of these weapons, with crews trained especially for the task. Indeed, crews flying the C-124s for SAC, AMC and AFLC included a position known as the "nuclear navigator." These specialist navigators were considered the best of the best, as they were responsible for flying extremely long distances with, arguably, the most dangerous cargo likely to be carried. One former nuclear navigator suggested the C-124s assigned to these units had the cargo floor reinforced. This may well account for the aircraft assigned to certain units retaining the special weapons mission rather than performing conventional airlift duties. However, there would seem no logic to the C-124s of the nuclear transportation units requiring extra reinforcement, as the weight of their load would unlikely be more than that originally catered for by the aircraft manufacturer.

Above: C-124Cs 52-0977 and 52-1020 of the 4th SSS during a deployment to the UK, probably sometime during the long hot summer of 1959. (via Terry Panopalis)

Left: Decorated with the stylized nose markings of the 3rd SSS, C-124A 49-0237 served briefly with SAC and MATS before becoming a ground trainer. (SAC)

SAC was anxious to conduct an overseas deployment performed entirely with "in house" assets to evaluate the success or failure of such an operation. Consequently, six Convair B-36D Peacemakers from the 7th and 11th BWs at Carswell AFB flew to Lakenheath on January 16, 1951. Support was provided by 2nd SSS C-124A 49-0236, 49-0237 and 49-0244, the first visit of the type to Europe. The Squadron had not yet been declared as combat ready, although the C-124s were crewed by experienced personnel who had sufficient skills in transport aircraft operations to undertake the exercise with confidence. While this deployment went ahead without incident, 49-0244 was lost on March 23, 1951, when the aircraft ditched in the Atlantic Ocean 450 miles west of Ireland while on an identical flight to Lakenheath. This was the first serious accident involving the Globemaster, with the loss of all 53 people on board including Brig Gen Paul T. Cullen.

Throughout the decade, SAC C-124s were commonplace visitors supporting the mass deployments of the huge number of strategic bomber squadrons worldwide. However, having transferred responsibility of the special weapons delivery to AMC, SAC eventually relinquished the intercontinental transportation mission to MATS, enabling the Command to concentrate on its core mission.

Above: A familiar image, but nevertheless historic, as 49-0244 was one of the first three C-124s to visit the UK, while supporting a B-36 deployment to RAF Lakenheath during January 1951. The aircraft disappeared on a flight across the Atlantic Ocean two months later, becoming the first Globemaster loss. (Quadrant)

Right: 49-0242 with the Milky Way sash applied but retaining the Arctic Red tail markings. The aircraft was with the 2nd SSS for its entire SAC career. (via Terry Panopalis)

For many years, C-124A 49-0258 was exhibited within the SAC Museum at Offutt AFB, where the aircraft is seen during February 1981. When the museum relocated the 30 miles to Ashland, Nebraska, the C-124 remained behind, but was later acquired by the Air Mobility Command Museum at Dover AFB. (Steve Hill)

Interestingly, the 3902nd ABW at Offutt AFB was briefly assigned 51-0078 during April and May 1952. The aircraft was assigned to the Air Proving Ground at Eglin AFB at the time, and was possibly demonstrating a new capability to SAC personnel. The 3902nd provided support for SAC headquarters, so was probably briefly assigned to the unit for convenience. Furthermore, 49-0258 was also allocated to the 3902nd when the aircraft was deleted from the inventory prior to being displayed with the SAC museum at Offutt AFB.

SSgt Ura Matthews recalls being the loadmaster on 49-0258 when it was flown to Nebraska in July 1969 for transfer to the museum:

Pilot Lt. Col Billy Morrison elected to give an impromptu display when we were on approach. I was sitting in the back scanning the right wing when the pilot said we were going to do a "pop-up." Billy was really enjoying showing off the capabilities, with the pop-up really making the C-124 shake like never before. The inside compartment buffeted and expanded over and over until we levelled out and started our approach again. Finally, the aircraft landed and was greeted by the Governor of Nebraska along with Air Force commanders and dignitaries. This was a fitting end to a varied career.

Tactical Air Command

TAC was another organization already established when the USAF became independent. While SAC was the long-range, strategic strike component, TAC was the close air support for the US Army. TAC flew the C-124 primarily to provide transportation for large numbers of troops and their equipment to be parachuted into combat zones or landed nearby. However, after six years these aircraft were transferred to MATS.

Right: 8th TCS C-124A 51-0099 parked at Boise Air Terminal, Idaho, during August 1952. The C-124 was one of three supporting the deployment of the resident Idaho ANG North American P-51Ds, which are in the distance beneath the Globie's nose. (William T Larkins)

Below: Six months after being delivered to the 15th TCS in April 1953, 51-7277 is seen on static display at Dayton, Ohio. (Bob Gerrard)

TAC C-124 assignments:

Assignment	Squadron	Base	Confirmed Dates
62nd TCW		McChord AFB	August 15, 1947, to April 20, 1952
		Larson AFB	April 21, 1952, to July 1, 1957 (transferred to MATS)
	61st TCG		September 30, 1946, to August 15, 1954
	62nd TCG		August 15, 1947, to July 1, 1957
	4th TCS		July 8, 1952, to July 1, 1957
	7th TCS		December 10, 1950, to July 1, 1957 (with 62nd TCG)
	8th TCS		May 28, 1951, to July 1, 1957 (with 62nd TCG)
	14th TCS		December 1, 1952, to August 25, 1954
	15th TCS		November 21, 1952, to August 25, 1954

Assignment	Squadron	Base	Confirmed Dates
63rd TCW		Altus MAP/AFB	January 8, 1953, to October 15, 1953
		Donaldson AFB	October 15, 1953, to July 1, 1957 (transferred to MATS)
	61st TCG		August 25, 1954, to June 30, 1957
	63rd TCG		June 27, 1949, to July 1, 1957
	64th TCG		October 15, 1953 to February 15, 1954
	3rd TCS		June 20, 1953, to July 1, 1957
	9th TCS		June 20, 1953, to July 1, 1957
	14th TCS		August 25, 1954, to July 1, 1957
	15th TCS		August 25, 1954, to July 1, 1957
	52nd TCS		March 19, 1953, to July 1, 1957
	53rd TCS		November 21, 1952, to July 1, 1957
	54th TCS		July 23, 1956, to July 1, 1957

TAC took delivery of its first Globemaster on December 10, 1950, when 49-0252 joined the 7th TCS, 62nd TCG, at McChord AFB. The initial delivery was a gigantic improvement compared with aircraft types that had served previously with the Group as well as the Command. TAC commanders were

Above: 7th TCS C-124A 51-0094 at Mitchell Field in November 1953. (John D R Rawlings)

Left: Wearing the Wolf in Sheep's Clothing emblem of the 3rd TCS, an unidentified C-124 is unloading a large wooden crate through the clam shell doors.

Above: 51-5209 of the 52nd TCS during the mid-1950s, shortly before the aircraft was absorbed into MATS. (The Aviation Photo Company)

Right: A 9th TCS C-124 at Donaldson AFB, South Carolina, during 1956. The nose markings on TAC C-124s were stylish and individual, but were all consigned to history when their aircraft was absorbed into MATS in 1957.

sceptical the type would be of use, and initially reluctant to accept deliveries, although they were soon won over. Other C-124s joined TAC, before the first examples began to be received by MATS in substantial numbers from 1951.

Whereas MATS C-124s had a global mission delivering cargo to numerous destinations, those with TAC were primarily to support the Army. TAC also flew sorties in support of humanitarian emergencies. During the 1954 French Indochina War, the Vietnamese forces eventually defeated the French. Relying heavily upon US support, TAC C-124s were engaged in transporting wounded French troops back to their home country.

The introduction of the extremely versatile Lockheed C-130 Hercules into TAC service beginning in 1957 enabled the DoD to implement a reorganization of airlift assets. The C-130 was more suited to delivering troops close to the combat zone, with the added feature of the ability to adopt short field landing on unpaved surfaces. Therefore, strategic airlift was reorganized, with some 130 TAC C-124s being transferred to MATS on July 1, 1957.

Despite no longer being a C-124 operator, TAC was allocated as the gaining command for five CONAC reserve squadrons called to active service for the period October 1, 1961, to August 27, 1962. This was due to the all too familiar escalation in tension as Soviet Union officials laid barbed wire as a prelude to constructing the Berlin Wall in August 1961. Note, a gaining command was the active duty organization, which was responsible for reservists mobilized by the DoD during times of emergency.

The 435th and 463rd TCWs were located at Homestead AFB, Florida, and Sewart AFB, Tennessee, respectively, with responsibility for the C-124 squadrons as geographically separated units for the 11 months of activation. These units were prepared for active duty, if necessary, in response to the Berlin Wall construction.

Assignment	Squadron	Base
435th TCW	78th TCS	Barksdale AFB
442nd TCW	303rd TCS	Grandview AFB, KS
	304th TCS	
	305th TCS	Tinker AFB
463rd TCW	77th TCS	Donaldson AFB

After almost a year, with the situation less volatile, the five squadrons returned to federal service, although with only half of the number of C-124s that were originally mobilized – the remainder were retained by the active duty.

Airlift Assignments in July 1962
On July 31, 1962, there were 397 aircraft assigned for airlift duties, composed of 175 C-124A models, and 222 C-124Cs. These were allocated as follows:

MATS

Unit	Base	C-124A	C-124C
62nd TCW	McChord	41	-
63rd TCW	Donaldson	31	30
	Rhein-Main	-	13
1501st ATW	Travis	21	18
	Hill	-	16
1502nd ATW	Hickam	19	1
1503rd ATW	Tachikawa	26	-
1607th ATW	Dover	-	54
1608th ATW	Charleston	-	43
1707th ATW	Tinker	-	9
CONAC but mobilized to TAC			
435th TCW	Barksdale	9	-
	Donaldson	6	-
442nd TCW	Richards-Gebaur	15	-
	Tinker	7	-
AFLC			
7th LSS	Robins	-	18
19th LSS	Kelly	-	20
Total		175	222

Chapter 3

The Reserves

The reserves operated the C-124 for 13 years; initially, this was to augment the active duty with a small number of aircraft, but eventually more than half of the total production was assigned. It is almost certain that the C-124's service was extended due to the insatiable airlift requirement in support of combat operations in SEA. Whereas the active duty could provide much of the airlift capability to the war, the ANG and CONAC/AFRES supplemented the need by performing an annual two-week active-duty commitment flying a cargo mission to SEA. The slow C-124 took two weeks to complete a journey to South Vietnam and return, whereas the new Lockheed C-141 could accomplish

Right: It is almost possible to hear the brakes squealing and the Wasp engines ticking over as Utah ANG 52-0952 departs Salt Lake City Airport. (via EMCS)

Below: 52-1034 of the Tennessee ANG at Memphis in August 1972. The aircraft was retired to MASDC the following month. (Peter Berganini)

this in less than a week, especially once the "stage system" had been introduced, whereby replacement aircrews were in position at air bases across the Pacific Ocean to continue the sortie once the incoming aircraft personnel went into crew rest. The C-124 was eventually part of this same rapid cargo-movement process, reducing delivery time significantly.

CONAC was the controlling organization for the AFRES along with an input into the activities of the ANG. Both the ANG and CONAC/AFRES were constituted as legal entities, with the former established under State control, whereas the latter was federally organized.

Continental Air Command

CONAC was formed on December 1, 1948, primarily to fulfil an airlift role. CONAC was organized with dozens of individual squadrons administered by a numbered Group, with several Groups coordinated under a numbered Wing. Each Group or a pair of Groups were located at different military air bases or civilian airports, usually within a geographical area. The concept was known as detached status, and offered several advantages as the local community would more readily accept small units, while recruiting and maintaining manning levels created jobs for the local community. CONAC units were established primarily to be activated to bolster regular forces in times of crisis or wartime.

CONAC received its first C-124As in 1961. According to CONAC (and AFRES from August 1968), the annual C-124 totals were as follows:

1961	1962	1963	1964	1965	1966	1967	1968	1969	1970	1971	1972
45	28	20	20	29	105	158	118	115	136	100	21

The totals are interesting as they show the five squadrons of nine aircraft each in FY 1961, decreasing significantly for the next four years, as squadrons were mobilized to active duty during the 1961 Berlin

C-124A 49-0248 joined Continental Air Command (CONAC) in July 1965 when assigned to the 935th TCG at Richards-Gebaur AFB, where the image was taken in September 1967. (Clyde Gerdes).

50-0115 taking off from Prestwick Airport, UK, with the standard white upper fuselage and Day-Glo orange nose banding. The lack of any command or unit insignia would suggest the aircraft was transitioning from the active duty to CONAC, circa 1961. (The Aviation Photo Company)

Right: Throughout the early period of CONAC operations, the C-124s displayed the Group identity on the nose wheel door. However, this was changed to Wing title when the Group system was abolished. 49-0256 has "442nd MAW" in place of the "935th MAG."

Below: C-124A 50-0116 of 940th MAG at McClellan AFB departing Hickam AFB while conducting a resupply flight to South Vietnam during 1968. Note the unusual color scheme, probably during the transition from CONAC to AFRES. (Nick Williams)

crisis. Following the return to reserve status, the number increased from 1966 and peaked in 1968, when 20 squadrons were equipped with the C-124.

On October 1, 1961, all five C-124 squadrons were mobilized for assignment to TAC, consisting of three from the 435th and two from the 442nd TCW. The squadrons were relocated to active-duty bases, including Donaldson AFB. Interestingly, the five squadrons were partway through transitioning from the C-119 to the C-124A and had yet to complete the conversion. Nevertheless, the USAF needed the additional troop-carrier capability, with the units learning their new equipment while routinely flying sorties locally. With the crisis largely averted, the squadrons were relieved from the active duty on August 27, 1962. Eight CONAC Wings were again mobilized for the October 1962 Cuban Missile Crisis, but none were equipped with the C-124. Nevertheless, some CONAC C-124s were retained on active duty.

The first CONAC C-124A was 49-0233, which was transferred from the 62nd TCW at McChord AFB on January 20, 1961. CONAC/AFRES units that flew the Globemaster were:

Assignment	Squadron	Base	Confirmed Dates
901st MAG	731st MAS	Hanscom AFB	October 1966 to November 1972
904th MAG	336th MAS	Stewart AFB	July 1966 to January 1970
		Hamilton AFB	November 1969 to May 1972
905th MAG	337th MAS	Westover AFB	March 1966 to April 1972
909th MAG	756th MAS	Andrews AFB	July 1966 to August 1971
911th MAG	758th MAS	Pittsburgh IAP	October 1966 to April 1972
915th TCG	76th TCS	Homestead AFB	December 1965 to April 1966
	79th MAS	Homestead AFB	March 1966 to October 1971
916th TCG	77th TCS	Carswell AFB	January 1963 to July 1972
917th TCG*	78th TCS	Barksdale AFB	April 1961 to April 1972
918th TCG	700th TCS	Dobbins AFB	June 1965 to April 1972
921st MAG	67th MAS	Kelly AFB	May 1966 to July 1971
932nd MAG	73rd MAS	Scott AFB, IL	January 1967 to August 1969
935th TCG*	303rd TCS	Richards-Gebaur AFB	December 1961 to August 1971
936th TCG*	304th TCS	Richards-Gebaur AFB	May 1961 to October 1971
937th TCG*	305th TCS	Tinker AFB	January 1961 to May 1972
938th MAG	312th MAS	Hamilton AFB	May 1966 to June 1969
940th TCG	314th TCS	McClellan AFB	June 1965 to June 1972
941st TCG	97th TCS	McChord AFB	July 1965 to May 1969
942nd TCG	728th TCS	March AFB	August 1965 to December 1971
945th MAG	733rd MAS	Hill AFB	June 1966 to November 1972

Units marked with an * transitioned to the C-124 before the Group system was restarted.

Note units were designated as TCG/TCSs until January 1966, when they changed to MAG/MAS to correspond with the new MAC designation system. Earlier, in 1957, the TCG system was inactivated, with the squadrons reporting directly to the Wing, despite flying activities being spread across several bases through the "Detached Squadron Concept." However, the two mobilizations in 1961 and 1962 highlighted a significant problem recalling an entire Wing to active duty. Beginning late in 1962 and into 1963, CONAC began reforming the structure by reintroducing the Group arrangement between the Squadron and Wing. The new structure enabled the aircraft and/or the personnel alone to be mobilized, or any other combination as needed.

CONAC C-124A 50-0112 of the 940th MAG at Mather AFB, California, during May 1968. (Jay Sherlock)

51-0153 was stationed at March AFB with the 942nd MAG from October 1966, but displays the 452nd MAW title on the nose wheel door, as the aircraft was stationed at the Wing HQ. (via EMCS)

51-0138 departing Andrews AFB during September 1968 while serving with the resident 909th MAG. (Steve Miller)

After reverting from TAC back to reservist service in 1964, CONAC C-124C 49-0253 had a major overhaul, and is seen about to perform an air test ahead of having command titles reapplied.

In July 1963, MATS replaced TAC as the gaining command for reserve C-124 units when mobilized. The MATS Commander, Lt Gen Joe W Kelly, announced that he intended to integrate CONAC C-124 units into the worldwide network of routine airlift missions. CONAC began C-124 flights across the Pacific Ocean in September 1963. To enable these lengthy sorties to be effective, reservists assigned to a Category A unit, such as a TCS, were authorized 24 days of inactive duty and 15 days of active duty training annually. Aircrew were authorized a further 36 days inactive duty each year to enhance their flying skills.

The gradual build up of US forces in SEA resulted in an accumulation of cargo at the West Coast aerial ports. CONAC C-124s began increasing the number of trans-Pacific sorties from seven to 20 to help

With no insignia apart from the CONAC emblem on the rear fuselage, 49-0250 of the 935th MAG from Richards-Gebaur AFB visits Richmond, Australia, during June 1967. (Ben Dannecker)

Above: 51-0103 and 51-01080 await their next European sortie at RAF Mildenhall during the period when C-124s replaced the C-130 rotation in 1968 and 1969. (Lindsay Peacock)

Right: 51-5186 during mobilization and deployment to RAF Mildenhall during March 1969. (Lindsay Peacock)

alleviate this backlog. Sorties normally involved more than 75 flight hours each way. Most reserve sorties terminated in Japan, but from January 1965 these continued to destinations in SEA.

During 1968, five C-124 squadrons were recalled to active duty to replace Stateside-based tactical airlift units that had been urgently flown to Vietnam following an increase in combat activities by the Viet Cong and North Vietnamese. Amongst the C-130 units were the 39th TAS, 317th TAW, from Lockbourne AFB, which was on three-month temporary duty at RAF Mildenhall. When the C-130 squadron returned home on July 8, 1968, it was replaced in the UK by a complement of C-124Cs.

MAC activated the 1648th MAS (Provisional) at Mildenhall on July 8, 1968, although the first C-124C had arrived at the base three days earlier. Sixteen aircraft were in residence at any one time, with a total of 36 rotating during the 11 months of the operation. Aircraft temporarily rotated to the 1648th MAS were drawn from:

Assignment	Squadron	Base
904th MAG	336th MAS	Stewart AFB
918th MAG	700th MAS	Dobbins AFB
921st MAG	67th MAS	Kelly AFB
938th MAG	312th MAS	Hamilton AFB
941st MAG	97th MAS	McChord AFB

The CONAC/AFRES C-124s performed the majority of the missions in the same manner as those conducted by the active-duty C-130 Hercules squadrons. However, the C-124s did so at a much slower pace than the C-130s. The experience and dedication of the maintenance personnel ensured that repairs and servicing were carried out with the minimum of delay to the planned missions. The C-124s began leaving Mildenhall in May 1969, with the last departing for home on May 16. The Provisional Squadron was inactivated on May 25. The operation was a success and ensured that the C-124 accomplished another significant chapter in a momentous career.

Taxiing against a threatening black sky at RAF Mildenhall during December 1968, 51-0080 passes some resident C-47s while deployed to the UK. (Bob Archer)

On August 1, 1968, reserves units were reorganized, with HQ CONAC being discontinued, and AFRES being formed as a separate operating agency with procedures, functions and responsibilities of a major command.

Returning to Hamilton AFB, California, at the completion of mobilization with MAC, 51-0077 was one of 32 different C-124Cs that deployed to Mildenhall during the 11 months of active duty. (Jay Sherlock)

Throughout the period when the 1648th MAS was in residence, the rotational C-124s were parked on various aprons at Mildenhall. 51-0097 waits in the southwest corner six days before the final aircraft left on May 16, 1969. (Michael Thorne)

During the 11-month period that mobilized CONAC C-124s for MAC service at Mildenhall, other reservist aircraft also periodically visited. C-124C 49-0253 from the 935th MAG was in transit on 10 August 1968. "CAC" is still displayed within the tail stripe, despite the CONAC having been replaced by AFRES ten days earlier. (Michael Thorne)

Air Force Reserves

As stated previously, AFRES came into being on August 1, 1968, when CONAC was deactivated. Whereas CONAC had been primarily airlift-orientated, along with a number of air rescue squadrons, AFRES gradually expanded roles to encompass a wide variety of missions mirroring the ANG.

CONAC C-124 units had displayed the Command's emblem on the rear fuselage, the Group numerical identity on the nose wheel door, and the logo within the tail band, but these were soon replaced with AFRES titles.

During 1962, the reserves began the humanitarian mission Project *Navajo* into the Four Corners area to deliver hay and feed for livestock following an especially harsh winter. The unit continued its friendship with the Navajo, donating and delivering clothes, school supplies, and later deploying medical personnel to southern Utah to perform physical exams on 600 Navajo children. During 1970, C-124C 51-0082 was decorated with a stylized mural of the Advent of Christ painted by Navajo students from the Intermountain Indian School in Brigham City, Utah. (via Douglas M Ducote Sr)

C-124C 50-0085 of 442nd MAW parked next to the perimeter fence at RAF Mildenhall during October 1968. Seven months later, the aircraft was retired to MASDC and subsequently scrapped. (via EMCS)

Upon formation, AFRES had 40 airlift squadrons, the majority equipped with the Fairchild C-119 Boxcar, apart from 20 squadrons equipped with the C-124A and C models. At the time, AFRES Wings were responsible for Squadrons located at two or more locations, with a numbered Group forming the link between. As an example, the 442nd TCW had five squadrons at four bases, as follows:

77th TCS	916th TCG	Carswell AFB	C-124C
78th TCS	917th TCG	Barksdale AFB	C-124A
303rd TCS	935th TCG	Richards-Gebaur AFB	C-124C
304th TCS	936th TCG	Richards-Gebaur AFB	C-124C
305th TCS	937th TCG	Tinker AFB	C-124A

Right: **AFRES 51-0136 departing Mildenhall, circa 1970. Although CONAC was the main reservist operator of the C-124 initially, its aircraft rarely traveled to Europe until circa 1965/1966. But as soon as CONAC was replaced by AFRES, its operating area expanded greatly. (Fred Smith)**

Below: **An immaculate C-124C 51-5180 of the 932nd MAG at Scott AFB is statically exhibited at Davis-Monthan AFB air show during November 1968. (via EMCS)**

Despite performing exceptional service for more than a decade, the gradual reduction of US forces in SEA, along with the delivery of more capable jet airlifters enabled AFRES to retire their elderly transporters. Furthermore, the success of the Associate program, whereby AFRES personnel augmented its active duty counterparts, was expanded to include airlift units transitioning to the C-141 and later the C-5. One squadron relinquished the C-124 in 1966, three more in 1969, followed by six in 1971, and the remaining ten in 1972. The final AFRES C-124 to be retired was 52-1011 of the 945th MAG, which arrived with MASDC on 12 October 1972.

Looking in remarkably good external order, 52-1045 of the 918th MAG at Dobbins AFB is at Prestwick Airport during April 1971. (David Montgomery)

51-0085 arrived back at Hamilton AFB in February 1969 following a period of mobilization and deployment to Mildenhall with the 1648th MAS (Provisional). The aircraft rejoined the AFRES, as seen here in May 1970, serving with four different units before retirement in April 1972. (Phil Owen)

Air National Guard

The ANG was another organization that pre-dated the formation of the USAF. Whereas the AFRES was federally organized, the ANG had state responsibility. Both the AFRES and ANG could be mobilized in times of emergency.

Parked at Mildenhall in March 1973, on the apron that now hosts the Special Operations Command MC-130s, 52-1076 of the Oklahoma ANG was retired 16 month later despite appearing in immaculate condition. (Dave Wilton)

Taxiing at Yokota AB during February 1971, Mississippi ANG C-124C 53-0019 has a stylized rectangle containing the state details along the upper fuselage. (Akira Watanabe)

Assignment	Squadron	Base	Confirmed Dates
116th MAG	128th MAS	Dobbins AFB	December 1966 to December 1972
118th MAG	105th MAS	Nashville Airport	April 1967 to June 1971
137th MAG	185th MAS	Will Rogers World Airport	February 1968 to July 1974
138th MAG	125th MAS	Tulsa Airport	February 1968 to October 1972
145th MAG	156th MAS	Charlotte Airport, NC	December 1966 to July 1971
151st MAG	191st MAS	Salt Lake City Airport, UT	January 1969 to September 1972
157th MAG	133rd MAS	Pease AFB, NH	February 1968 to October 1971
164th MAG	155th MAS	Memphis Airport, TN	May 1967 to August 1974
165th MAG	158th MAS	Savannah Airport, GA	July 1967 to September 1974
172nd MAG	183rd MAS	Jackson Airport, MS	March 1967 to June 1972

The ANG followed a similar pattern to CONAC/AFRES, with the 128th MAS Georgia ANG at Dobbins AFB spearheading an eventual complement of ten squadrons. By late 1969, the reserves had 225 C-124s while the active duty had just nine. AFRES and the ANG gradually assumed a higher proportion of the airlift mission, a role that the units have continued subsequently.

Left: **One of the last Georgia ANG C-124s to visit Mildenhall was 52-1025, which is seen departing during early July 1972. It was retired days later, on July 24. (Bob Archer)**

Below: **53-0001 was originally delivered to the 15th ATS at Westover AFB on 16 September 1954. It later served with the 7th LSS at Robins AFB before joining the Georgia ANG.**

Right: Georgia ANG 53-0001 departs into the morning sunrise on yet another westbound resupply flight. The insatiable demands of the war in South East Asia ensured the C-124 squadrons were constantly in demand. (Nick Williams)

Below: The last C-124 to be processed into storage was 53-0044 of the Georgia ANG, which landed on September 19, 1974, and was allocated inventory number CQ364. It was subsequently flown to Las Vegas during November 1980 for display with a private owner. (Brian Rogers collection)

52-0953 of the Utah ANG making a resupply sortie to Los Angeles Air Force Station, located at the main international airport, circa 1969.

The ANG began operating the C-124 on December 7, 1966, when 53-0001 was delivered from the 58th MAS at Robins AFB to the 128th MAS at Dobbins AFB. The 156th MAS at Charlotte Airport began conversion the following week, when 53-0026 was also transferred from the 58th MAS. A further four units converted in 1967, followed by three more in 1968, and the final unit in 1969. The C-124 served faithfully with the ANG until September 19, 1974, when the 158th MAS at Savannah Airport flew its last two aircraft, serials 52-1066 and 53-0044, to storage with MASDC at Davis-Monthan AFB.

All ten squadrons were already performing the airlift role prior to receiving the C-124, and this meant the transition to the Globemaster was reasonably straightforward. In addition to augmenting active duty airlift squadrons, reserve component C-124 units were also integrated into the insatiable movement of cargo to the SEA area during the late 1960s and early 1970s. This included missions into the combat theater in the Republic of Vietnam.

ANG C-124s frequently departed their home station on a Saturday morning and flew to one of the active-duty airlift bases. Their cargo was loaded, and depending upon the remaining duty day the crew would commence its overseas flight. In the case of a European mission, this could well be to north-eastern Canada or the Azores. The second day would enable the crew to reach Europe, with RAF Prestwick or Mildenhall being frequent destinations, or other locations in West Germany and Spain also frequently being visited. From there, the aircraft could journey to many other European and Middle Eastern destinations, before beginning the journey home.

Left: Tennessee ANG C-124C 52-1044 about to depart Nashville Airport during August 1969. The aircraft went on to serve two AFRES Groups before joining the Tennessee ANG at Memphis Airport in October 1972. (Phil Owen)

Below: Despite the title "Air National Guard," all too often the word National was omitted when presented alongside the fuselage side. Here, Oklahoma ANG 52-1079 lands at Rhein-Main AB in 1970.

The wind down of westbound missions to SEA coincided with the completion of deliveries of the Lockheed C-5 Galaxy to MAC on May 3, 1973. The final flight by a C-124 was an ANG aircraft. C-124Cs 52-1000 of Oklahoma ANG and 53-0050 Utah ANG were both retired to Aberdeen Proving Ground, Maryland, sometime after June 1972.

North Carolina ANG C-124C 53-0013 parked at Richmond Airport in May 1967. The obligatory kangaroo zap has been applied to the nose wheel door and fuselage. (Ben Dannecker)

Another 1968 Hickam AFB departure, C-124C 53-0037 of the Georgia ANG transits between the US and the western Pacific. (Nick Williams)

Chapter 4

Operations

Operation *Deep Freeze*

The task to resupply the scientific community across the Antarctica continent was assigned to the US Navy during the austral summer of 1955/1956 under Operation *Deep Freeze*. However, it became apparent that large volumes of cargo, equipment, and machinery would be required, which could not be accommodated aboard the Douglas R5D Skymasters and Lockheed P2V Neptune's allocated to the program.

Therefore, for Operation *Deep Freeze II*, which commenced in September 1956, the 63rd TCW furnished eight C-124s. The Globemasters were modified with special compasses and navigation equipment, along with enhanced emergency power units. The 52nd TCS was selected to participate, as its crews had experience in ferrying supplies to Alaska, northern Canada and Greenland during the construction of the Distant Early Warning Line. Therefore, these units were familiar with operations onto snow-covered runways.

Towards the end of 1956, the C-124s were flown to Harewood Aerodrome, Christchurch, New Zealand, where a Detachment had been established to coordinate activities. Cargoes destined for Antarctica had been prepositioned at Christchurch. The main Antarctic landing strip was excavated at McMurdo Sound on the Ross Ice Shelf, although there were other small landing sites, as well as remote locations requiring aerial delivery.

The first C-124 to land on McMurdo Sound during *Deep Freeze II* was 51-5207 *Miss North Carolina*, which did so on October 21, 1956, bringing a de Havilland UC-1 Otter to perform localized resupply flights. Other C-124s landed without incident, although the ice runway gradually became rough and undulating. This caused the nose wheel to collapse when C-124 52-0983 *State of Washington* landed on November 28, seriously damaging the clam shell doors. Repairs were affected, and the aircraft returned to the US.

Above left: **52nd TCS C-124C 52-0983** *State of Washington* **following a landing accident at McMurdo Sound on November 28, 1956, which damaged the clam shell door. Replacements parts were flown in, and following repairs, the C-124 returned to service.**

Above right: **52nd TCS C-124 51-5207** *Miss North Carolina* **was the first C-124 to land at McMurdo Sound, bringing a de Havilland Otter on October 21, 1956. (USAF)**

The first C-124 resupply flight to the South Pole took place aboard 52-1015 *State of Oregon* on October 26, with an air drop of fuel and equipment. Sadly, 52-1015 hit a snowbank when landing on November 30, sheering the landing gear and causing a fire in the forward section. The aircraft was damaged beyond repair, with part of the fuselage later converted into a stores shed.

Deep Freeze II was the one and only occasion that TAC supported any part of the mission, as its two C-124 Wings were transferred to MATS in July 1957. *Deep Freeze III* was a MATS operation performed by the 63rd TCW with personnel formerly assigned to TAC. During the dozen or so weeks of C-124 sorties, 12 Wasp engines were replaced, including five at McMurdo Sound despite the harsh weather conditions. Most of the replacements were for C-124A models, so the decision was made to send only C models in the future. Antarctic operations were flown into largely uncharted territory, and the hazardous operations were again highlighted when C-124C 52-1017 *The City of Christchurch* struck an incorrectly charted mountain ridge near Cape Hallett on October 15, 1958, and was destroyed, with the loss of six of the 13 persons on board.

The involvement of the Globemaster community in *Deep Freeze II* was not a small undertaking. Some 300 personnel were forward deployed, backed up by more support at Donaldson AFB, the home station for the 63rd TCW. The distances involved were quite staggering. Each C-124 had to fly 2,300 nautical miles from Donaldson to Travis

Right: C-124 52-0990 *Preoria* unloading a bulldozer at McMurdo Sound during late-1956.

Below: 52-1008 of the 14th TCS was originally assigned to the 61st TCG, which was stationed at Larson AFB until the Group was transferred to Donaldson AFB. It is believed the aircraft was loaned to the 52nd TCS to participate in *Deep Freeze* in 1956.

AFB, then 2,142 to Hickam AFB, and 1,659 to Canton Island. The next stop was Fiji, 1,105 nautical miles further, before the final 1,570 to Christchurch, for a total of 8,776 miles – the equivalent to one-third of the way around the world. Each sortie to McMurdo Sound was 2,021 nautical miles, taking anything up to ten hours to achieve. Ordinarily, the aircraft would be unloaded fairly quickly, and after refueling, would return to New Zealand, thereby achieving an extremely long crew duty day.

Deep Freeze 63, which commenced on October 7, 1962, was the last occasion that C-124s participated in this large-scale resupply operation. The Navy had introduced a ski-equipped version of the C-130 Hercules, which although unable to accommodate the volume of cargo, nevertheless required less runway, was cheaper to operate, and was an overall improvement in capability. The USAF likewise introduced the C-130, rendering the C-124 redundant. However, the Globie still had valuable contributions to make, when a pair of 1608th ATW C-124s brought two US Army Bell UH-1B Iroquois to McMurdo Sound, in a mission that took 100 flying hours and ten days to complete. The C-124 was also employed one final time in October 1968, when a 436th MAW C-124C airlifted two UH-1Ds from Langley AFB to McMurdo.

During seven years of C-124 *Deep Freeze* operations, the Globies flew 431 airlift and 513 airdrop sorties, delivering hundreds of tons of supplies. Apart from the single mission by the 436th MAW, all the others were flown by the 63rd TCW.

Left: 63rd TCW 53-0031 at Christchurch Airport, New Zealand, during late 1961 while flying *Deep Freeze* missions to Antarctica. (Jack Friell collection)

Below: 63rd TCW C-124C 53-0052 at McMurdo Sound in November 1962. The aircraft was one of the last Globemasters to fly *Deep Freeze* missions between New Zealand and the Antarctic continent. (USAF)

Interestingly, the arrival of the C-124s in the southern hemisphere in October 1962 coincided with the discovery of vessels sailing to Cuba from the Soviet Union delivering an inordinate quantity of offensive weapons. The Cuban Missile Crisis affected all branches of the DoD, with the requirement for a massive increase in the relocation of forces to the south-eastern US. Airlift was a major feature, with hundreds of sorties to the region. Such was the need that half the C-124s dedicated to *Deep Freeze* operations were recalled back to the US. However, reorganizing the C-124s return took time, resulting in the aircraft landing at Hickam AFB just as the Cuban emergency was over!

Operations in Europe

The United States Air Forces in Europe (USAFE) was not assigned the C-124 directly, although the type was a prolific visitor during three decades of service. Furthermore, there were several occasions when the C-124 was operated within Europe for fairly lengthy periods supporting USAFE requirements, while remaining assigned to the parent organization at home. The 53rd TCS, which was assigned to the 61st Troop Carrier Group at Donaldson AFB, South Carolina, deployed to Rhein-Main AB under Airlift Task Force, Provisional. The 16 C-124s were in residence between August 1958 and February 1959; February and July 1960; and again from early January 1961 until April 1962. The squadron was reassigned to the 63rd TCG (later Wing) in October 1959, but without relocating from its home station. The 29 months spent in Europe were primarily to bolster airlift capability during periods of world tension. The first was in response to the Lebanon crisis in mid-1958, the second after Cuba's chilling of relations with the US, and the third during strained relations with the Soviet Union over Berlin. These deployments were in addition to the 52nd TCS, which was deployed to Rhein-Main from January to August 1960, and again from January 1962 until inactivated on February 8, 1969. Throughout this period, the squadron remained assigned to the parent unit in the US.

In July 1968, RAF Mildenhall had two rotational C-130 squadrons totaling 32 aircraft from the US at any one time. However, the insatiable requirement for tactical airlift in SEA was such that the 39th TAS, 317th TAW, flying the C-130A was withdrawn from the UK and returned to the US to enable a Stateside

A group of mobilized CONAC personnel shortly after arriving at RAF Mildenhall in July 1968.

C-130E unit to be added to the SEA commitment. To make up the shortfall in capacity for the ongoing airlift requirement within Europe, the Air Force mobilized AFRES C-124Cs drawn from five units:

Assignment	Squadron	Base
904th MAG	336th MAS	Stewart AFB
918th MAG	700th MAS	Dobbins AFB
921st MAG	67th MAS	Kelly AFB
938th MAG	312th MAS	Hamilton AFB
941st MAG	97th MAS	McChord AFB

51-5175 was temporarily based at Mildenhall when seen departing Tempelhof Airport during July 1968. With power set to maximum during take-off, the sound of the Wasps was the most magnificent roar, which could make the ground vibrate. (Peter Seemann)

Taxiing at Rhein-Main AB during January 1969, 349th MAW C-124C 51-0074 was deployed to RAF Mildenhall with the 1648th MAS (Provisional). (Lindsay Peacock)

Above: Surrounded by unseasonal snow at RAF Mildenhall during April 1969, C-124C 51-0129 shortly before returning to the US on the completion of the period of mobilization. (Lindsay Peacock)

Right: One of the last aircraft to leave Mildenhall at the completion of ten months' deployment, 51-0132 departed in May 1969 just before the 1648th MAS was deactivated. (via EMCS)

As previously mentioned, the 1648th MAS (Provisional) was formed at Mildenhall on July 8, 1968, and was in situ until inactivated on May 25, 1969. C-124C 51-5175 arrived on July 5, followed by 15 more C-124s within two weeks. Throughout the 11 months in residence, the C-124s flew to all the US military facilities in Europe as well as certain allied nations in the Middle East and North Africa. However, with the SEA situation stabilizing, the Hercules commitment to Europe resumed, permitting the C-124s to return to their reserve status. The last aircraft to depart was 51-5181 on May 16, 1969. The C-124 contingent was replaced by C-130Es of the 777th TAS, 464th TAW, from Pope AFB, North Carolina.

Operation *Big Lift*

The US Armed Forces frequently respond to world crises or humanitarian requests. Intervention on an international scale has usually required the reinforcement of an area with additional forces, most frequently involving airlifting of assets. Throughout the Cold War period, barely a year passed without the US conducting such a response, either on a military footing, or through humanitarian aid. To ensure that units were familiar with the procedures and could deploy and be ready for any contingency quickly and effectively, exercises were staged to provide familiarity, and to highlight shortcomings that could be rectified in peacetime. The active duty USAF units frequently accomplished training for many different contingencies, primarily to ensure that personnel were capable of performing their operational role successfully. The ANG and CONAC/AFRES were similarly trained, although being predominantly part-time staffed, this was a little more difficult. Regardless, however, such training for the reserves was performed during the annual two-week "drill period."

Above left: 52-0980 of the 63rd TCW was one of over 100 C-124s that participated in Operation *Big Lift* in October 1963. It is seen transiting Prestwick Airport on the return journey. (Eric Roscoe)

Above right: 1607th ATW 52-1007 was also a participant in *Big Lift*. (Tom Hildreth)

The division across Europe between the forces of NATO and those of the Warsaw Pact, was defined by Winston Churchill as the "iron curtain." All too often the Soviet Union tested Western resolve with a sudden act of provocation that could possibly have escalated into full-scale war, and almost invariably the incident was staged within the segregated city of Berlin. The US response was to reinforce the already massive troop concentration in West Germany, while strengthening aviation elements with additional fighter squadrons in Western Europe. Following several minor confrontations, and the construction of the Berlin Wall, the US DoD organized a massive peacetime deployment exercise for late 1963. The plan was to rapidly move an entire Armored Division from the US to West Germany, although the equipment and supplies had been prepositioned via embarkation seaports located in various adjacent countries.

Then came the speedy airlift of the troops from their home garrisons to air bases conveniently close to the central plains of West Germany. Hundreds of tanks, armoured pieces, support equipment, and virtually everything necessary to sustain a combat operation for an entire Division sailed from ports in Texas to Europe during the summer months of 1963, and was delivered by rail, road and barge to forward-staging areas. Much of this hardware was lined up on disused autobahns. The reuniting of the forward-deployed equipment with the troops was seen as a "marriage," to quote the popular term in vogue at the time.

The aviation role was named Operation *Big Lift*, and was sponsored by United States Strike Command, designed to demonstrate the military capability to airlift a large force of US Army personnel in the shortest possible time. *Big Lift* appealed to Defense Secretary Robert McNamara as he was particularly interested in the potential cost savings from being able to reduce the large Army presence in Europe. In the event of tension, the troops stationed in West Germany could be quickly reinforced, thereby offering a vast saving in the European defence budget.

MATS was responsible for moving 15,358 officers and men, and more than 500 tons (453 tonnes) of equipment between October 22 and 24, 1963. The majority of troops were from the 2nd AD stationed at Fort Bliss, Texas. Six support Army units were also involved, including transportation elements from Fort Benning, Georgia, Fort Bragg, North Carolina, Fort Campbell, Kentucky, and Fort Eustis, Virginia, along with two artillery companies from Fort Sill, Oklahoma.

An advanced party of 500 key Army personnel had deployed from Bergstrom AFB, Texas aboard seven Boeing C-135 Stratolifters on October 19. The main body of the operation commenced with a C-135 departing Bergstrom AFB shortly after midnight local time on October 22, containing Major General Edwin Burba, the commanding officer of the 2nd AD, and his staff. The C-135 touched down at Ramstein AB as the first of more than 200 airlifters that would arrive in Europe during the next two and a half days.

The 2nd AD was airlifted from Bergstrom AFB, James Connally AFB, and Gray Army Airfield, while the two artillery units began their journey from Sheppard AFB. The transportation units utilized Langley AFB, Pope AFB, Campbell Army Airfield, Kentucky, and Lawson Army Airfield, Georgia. The final *Big Lift* aircraft sortie reached its off-load destination on October 24, to give an elapsed time of 63 hours and 5 minutes, which was well within the 72 hours specified by Strike Command.

The airlift utilized 23 C-135s, which mostly accomplished the flight from Texas to Germany non-stop in approximately 11 hours. Several of the aircraft performed two round trips during the 63-hour deployment phase. The C-135s carried 75 troops along with their baggage, which was restricted to their immediate needs. The primary destination for these aircraft was Ramstein and Rhein-Main ABs. The bulk of the airlift was performed by almost 100 Douglas C-124 Globemasters, which were drawn primarily from regular stateside-based ATS and TCSs, although at least three were from the 1502nd ATW at Hickam AFB. Most of these aircraft took three times as long to complete their journey as their jet-powered contemporaries. Other airlift types supporting the operation exclusively were 35 Douglas C-118A Liftmasters, 30 Lockheed C-130E Hercules, and 23 Douglas C-133 Cargomasters. Three quarters of the C-124s transited RAF Mildenhall, where tented facilities catered for thousands of troops and crew members. The base also provided fuel and servicing for the aircraft, as well as billeting for 600 aircrew. Many of the C-118s also transited facilities in northeast Canada, Kindley Field, Bermuda, Lajes AB, Azores, and Prestwick Airport, Scotland. The Canadian bases also supported the other short-range types, such as the C-130. Again the majority of these aircraft were destined for Rhein-Main and Ramstein.

In addition to the large Army contingent, there was a Composite Air Strike Force (CASF) from TAC fighter and tactical reconnaissance types, supported by 50 TAC Lockheed C-130 Hercules. Once in theater, the deployed forces participated in a week-long NATO exercise that simulated an attack along the border between East and West Germany. Having completed their part of the exercise, the C-124s and other transport elements gradually returned home.

Airlift Rodeo

For several decades, the USAF organized a competition to evaluate various aspects of airlift. Despite several official titles, the event was universally known as Rodeo. CONAC had the idea to organize a Reserve Troop Carrier Rodeo to evaluate aerial delivery techniques between units. The first event was staged at Bakalar AFB, Indiana, in October 1956, involving 13 units flying the Curtis C-46 Commando and Fairchild C-119 Flying Boxcar. TAC units were invited as guests, including some flying the C-124. Nine months later, MATS absorbed TAC's 100+ C-124s into the Service. The Eisenhower Administration recommended that MATS change its mission from a passenger service to a strictly military airlift organization, incorporating all tactical US Army deployments. Subsequently, the Kennedy Administration further stressed the importance of rapid global mobility to respond to any problem at any spot on the globe at a moment's notice. The President wanted the US to have the capability to prevent both limited and guerrilla wars by being able to rapidly deploy military forces around the world. Until this time, MATS had only required troop-carrier units equipped with C-124s to be qualified in its Computed Air Release Point (CARP) aerial delivery technique. CARP required the aircrew to file a detailed flight plan with the exact "Time on Target." Using the CARP process correctly would ensure that an airdrop would be made on time and take place even if at night or if the drop zone was obscured by bad weather. Beginning in January 1961, MATS required all C-124 units to become CARP qualified.

The first "Rodeo" staged at Bakalar AFB, Indiana, in October 1956, was primarily for medium-category troop-carrier squadrons, but attracted several of TAC's C-124 units. 53rd TCS C-124 51-5176 is parked alongside other participants.

CARP Rodeo

Armed with this new direction, in April 1961, the Commander of the 1501st ATW, Richard Bromiley, proposed a command-wide CARP Rodeo as a method of enhancing airlift accuracy. While MATS was planning the details of such a competition, the Western Transport Air Force held its own CARP Rodeo between the 1501st ATW and the 62d TCW. On July 11, 1961, three crews from each wing flew low-level navigation routes and dropped miniature parachutes over part of Winters-Davis airstrip near Travis AFB. The 1501st won the competition over the 62nd, despite the latter having more experience with CARP.

Meanwhile, MATS was planning an annual, command-wide competition, the first held at Scott AFB between April 16 and 22, 1962. Seven Wings, the 62nd and 63rd TCWs, and the 1501st, 1502nd 1503rd, 1607th and 1608th ATWs, each sent one aircraft and two crews to participate. This first official CARP Rodeo consisted of three events: a low-level, daylight, navigational mission; a similar night mission; and a second daylight mission following a different route. During each mission, the team dropped a 25oz (0.7kg) shot bag attached to a miniature parachute simulating a 225lb (102kg) load. During the night missions, a small flashlight taken from a "Mae West" life preserver was attached to aid in recovery. Combat Control teams from the 62nd and 63rd Wings were stationed at the drop zones to recover and score drop accuracy.

On April 1, 1963, MATS required all units with airdrop capability to train formation flying, involving the aerial delivery of personnel and equipment using CARP. This directive, coupled with MATSs desire to add realism, led to the inclusion of formation flying, heavy cargo drops, and troop drops. Because of the unavailability of a suitable drop zone for heavy cargo and paratroops near Scott AFB, the second competition was held at Dover AFB, during the period September 22–28. The same seven wings participated again, with two crews and one C-124. However, both the 1501st and 1608th also entered a C-130 Hercules team. Each crew flew a morning, afternoon, and night cargo drop. Additionally, each crew was required to drop an Army team from the 101st Airborne Division over Fort Campbell. The Wings also sent a ten-man maintenance team, although its performance was not part of the competition.

The third CARP Rodeo, held from November 9–13, 1964, at Hunter AFB, expanded to include nine wings, including C-130 teams from the Naval Air Transport Wing, Atlantic and Pacific. The competition followed the same format as the previous year's, using drop zones on Fort Stewart. The MATS Commander, Gen Howell M. Estes II, named the trophies awarded in 1964 after former MATS commanders: the Lieutenant General Laurence S Kuter Trophy was awarded to the C-124 team with the highest aggregate score; the Lieutenant General Joseph Smith Trophy went to the C-130 team with the highest aggregate score; the

A trio of C-124Cs 51-0130, 51-0129 and 51-0102 of 1502nd ATW, at low level over the Pacific Ocean during 1964, practising parachute delivery techniques such as CARP. (USAF)

Lieutenant General William H Tunner Trophy went to the team, C-124 or C-130, with the best single drop; and the General Joe W Kelly Trophy was awarded the best crew, either C-124 or C-130.

The involvement in the Vietnam War escalated to such a degree that no Rodeo competitions were held after 1964. The new MAC wished to reintroduce the event, which it did in 1969. However, by this time, the active duty had all but relinquished the C-124, with no more involvement by the type.

Shortcomings

Routine sorties by the major Commands illustrated a number of shortcomings. In particular, the C-124 gained a reputation of not being powered by the most reliable engines, as the Wasp Majors regularly suffered from breakdowns. Furthermore, the lack of pressurization forced the C-124 to routinely fly at a cruising altitude of 10,000ft (3,048m). At this height, the aircraft was in the lower atmosphere, where turbulence was a problem, resulting in a bumpy ride for crew and passengers. Additionally, the Globemaster suffered from icing problems, with a build up on the wings and clamshell doors. It was not uncommon for the flight engineer and crew chief to try to remove ice by kicking the inside of the giant doors. One former C-124 crew member also vividly recalled watching the huge clam shell doors buckling as the aircraft flew though a tropical storm!

436th MAW 52-1007 landed at Atsugi Naval Base, Japan, in 1968 with an oil leak on one of the engines. (Nick Williams)

RAF Mildenhall had an apron located adjacent to the perimeter fence for many years, which afforded a wonderful view of parked aircraft, although this is no longer usable. Seen in April 1972, Tennessee ANG C-124C 52-0950 has a wheeled trolley positioned alongside to enable the flight engineer to inspect the Wasp engines. (via EMCS)

Chapter 5
Retirement

The first Globemaster to be retired to the MASDC at Davis-Monthan AFB was NC-124C 52-1069, which had arrived shortly before being authorized for reclamation on August 4, 1958. Gradually, the aircraft was stripped of reusable parts, with the carcass still present in 1968, although it is believed to have been scrapped the following year.

No further aircraft were retired until January and February 1967, when eight 1949-production C-124As were processed into MASDC for storage. Two years later, 131 C-124 airframes were flown to MASDC. During 1970, just 12 were retired, while in 1971 a further 76 were stored. During 1972, 1973 and 1974, MASDC received 97, 10 and 29 aircraft, respectively. MASDC processed a total of 364 aircraft, which includes two that were briefly returned to service and one that was displayed at the nearby Pima County Air Museum for a short time. All three later returned to MASDC.

Left: At the completion of the T57 development program, the test NC-124C 52-1069 was retired to MASDC by August 1958, and was still present ten years later. (Steve Miller)

Below: Completely devoid of any unit or command markings, C-124C 49-0252 shortly after arriving into MASDC on November 14, 1969. (Lindsay Peacock)

The last C-124Cs in operational flying status were 52-1066 and 53-0044 of 165th MAG, Georgia ANG, which were retired to Davis-Monthan on September 19, 1974. Of those which arrived by 1971, most were scrapped the following year, while the later arrivals had all been broken up and melted down for recycling by 1976. A great many of the earlier retirements were cannibalized for spare parts, especially their wheels and tyres, with row upon row of airframes sitting on their rear fuselages with their wheels missing.

The eighth Globemaster to enter MASDC was 49-0236, which was stored briefly before being allocated to the Pima County Air Museum. However, 49-0236 was replaced by C-124C 52-1004, returned to storage, and was subsequently scrapped. The aircraft is seen on static display at Davis-Monthan AFB during March 1968.

Right: Seen taxiing into MASDC for storage, which was a common occurrence at the time, although latterly aircraft were parked on the main flightline at Davis-Monthan AFB, and later towed to the storage area. AFRES C-124A 50-1263 is seen arriving into MASDC on November 18, 1969. (Lindsay Peacock)

Below: 51-0152 heads a row of C-124s that have had the engines removed, affecting the centre of gravity and causing the aircraft to sit on their rear fuselages. They are at MASDC during October 1975, shortly before the aircraft were scrapped. (Lou Pelham)

An anonymous C-124 being dismantled for melting down and recycling at MASDC on November 19, 1973. Note that all insignia and lettering has been over painted in black by the contractor. (Richard Lockett)

Left: **The penultimate C-124C to visit Mildenhall was 52-1042 of the Oklahoma ANG, which was present on 7 April 1974.**

Below: **The last C-124 to visit the UK was Oklahoma ANG 52-1029, which arrived on April 25, 1974, and departed soon afterwards. After returning home, the aircraft was retired to MASDC in June. It is seen at Will Rogers World Airport in August 1973. (Ron Munroe)**

Having been a prolific visitor to the UK since the first in 1951, the last two C-124s to transit RAF Mildenhall were from the Oklahoma ANG. 52-1042 arrived on April 7, 1974, followed on April 25 by 52-1029. These aircraft performed the final ANG sorties around Europe, before returning to Will Rogers World Airport at Oklahoma City a few days later. On June 25, 1974, 52-1029 made its final flight to Davis-Monthan, where after processing; it became the 338th for storage, joining rows of other Globemasters awaiting their fate. On 15 November 1974, it was declared excess, and struck off charge. Shortly afterward, the aircraft was scrapped and melted down to be recycled. 52-1042 followed on July 3, 1974, and was struck off charge on November 15, 1974.

An unidentified TAC C-124 of the 53rd TCS after having crashed some time prior to July 1957. This image has often been attributed to 50-0088, which is incorrect, as that aircraft was SAC-owned at the time of the loss on January 27, 1957, whereas the C-124 depicted is a TAC aircraft. (USAF)

Fate of the Fleet

Apart from those retired to MASDC, of the 448 C-124s 63 were lost to accidents or damaged beyond economical repair. The remaining dozen aircraft were either tested to destruction by the Federal Aviation Administration, or retired for miscellaneous purposes and eventually broken up for scrap.

MASDC Pictorial

The vast majority of C-124s were retired within a five-year window. And within two years of the final C-124 arriving the last of the 364 aircraft were sold for scrap. A selection of images are presented.

Right: 945th MAG C-124C 51-0105 is in a sorry state with engines and nose wheels removed at MASDC during October 1975. (Lou Pelham)

Below: 52-0992 was retired by the Georgia ANG, shortly after arriving at MASDC for store on November 22, 1972.

52-1085 was retired to MASDC by the Oklahoma ANG during February 1970, and was on display at the open day the following month. Within two years, the aircraft was scrapped and recycled. (via EMCS)

Above: ANG C-124 tails headed by Georgia ANG 52-1086 at MASDC during June 1975. No components had been removed at this time, although soon afterward these Globemasters were sold for scrap.

Below: Mississippi ANG C-124C 53-0002 resting on the rear fuselage at MASDC in October 1975. It was retired on June 8, 1972, and broken up in 1976. (Lou Pelham)

Right: C-124C 53-0045 of the Georgia ANG stored at MASDC during October 1975 minus the nose wheels. Replacement tyres were sought after, with the entire wheel assembly being removed and shipped to operational bases. (Lou Pelham)

Below: After many years detached to Rhein-Main AB for European operations, which ended in January 1969, 52-0956 was transferred to the Utah ANG, ahead of joining the Georgia ANG in August 1972. Four months later, the aircraft was retired to MASDC, where it is seen in October 1973. (Bob Archer)

Preserved C-124s

Nine C-124s are displayed in museums, with all except one located in the United States. Details as follows:

- 49-0258 was transferred to the SAC Museum at Offutt AFB in July 1969. When the exhibits were relocated to the new site at Ashland, Nebraska, in 1998, the C-124 was abandoned. However, the aircraft was reallocated to the Air Mobility Command Museum at Dover AFB, and following being disassembled beginning in 2002, it was moved by C-5s to Dover. Volunteers reassembled and repainted the aircraft, after which it joined the other exhibits outside.
- 51-0089 was retired on August 27, 1971, and flown to Harlingen Airport for storage with the Confederate Air Force (CAF). Due to the CAF being unable to maintain the aircraft, it was transferred in sections to the Museum of Aviation at Robins AFB by October 1986.
- 52-0943 was struck off charge at Will Rogers World Airport on January 12, 1974, and flown to South Korea for display at the Museum of the Military Academy, later renamed the Aero Space Museum, at Sacheon Airport.

51-0089 was donated to the Confederate Air Force (CAF) for its display of Cold War hardware, arriving soon after being SOC on August 27, 1971. However, personnel at Harlingen Airport were focussed on the upkeep of their World War Two aircraft, resulting in the C-124 suffering from the elements. 51-0089 is seen at Harlingen during September 1974.

Above: After having spent years parked at Harlingen Airport, Texas, 51-0089 was rescued and transported to Robins AFB for its Museum of Aviation. The aircraft is seen being re-assembled during October 1987. (Paul Bigelow)

Below: Wearing the emblem of the 7th LSS and the color scheme of AMC, 51-0089 is on display at Robins AFB Museum of Aviation. This C-124 is exhibited with authentic markings from the late 1950s/early 1960s.

Five months before being SOC and donated to the museum in Korea, 52-0943 is on the main ramp at Will Rogers World Airport during August 1973. (Ron Monroe)

Right: Wearing tail markings that are not strictly authentic, former Oklahoma ANG C-124C 52-0943 is on display at the Museum of the Military Academy in Seoul, South Korea. On a personal note, this was one of two last C-124s that I saw fly when they departed Norton AFB and overflew nearby Chino, California, while I was visiting in October 1973.

Below: One of only nine C-124s to survive into display, 52-0994 of the 1607th ATW is at Rhein-Main AB in July 1962.

- 52-0994 was stuck off charge in Savannah, Georgia, on January 16, 1973, and flown to Willow Run Airport with registration N86599, then allocated for display with the Detroit Institute of Aeronautics. However, the aircraft was acquired by the McChord Air Museum, which prepared the aircraft for a flight to Selfridge ANG Base, Michigan. The aircraft was refurbished by volunteers prior to making the 2,350-mile (3,780km) flight to McChord AFB on October 8, 1986. This is the last recorded flight of a C-124. Prior to landing at McChord, the Globemaster was joined by a C-130E and a C-141 from the resident 62nd MAW for a formation flypast. The C-124 was subsequently repainted in a colorful scheme before being moved during January 2005 to its present position in the Heritage Park.

In the final Globemaster flight, 52-0994 lands at McChord AFB on October 9, 1986, to be preserved with the base's museum. (Doug Remington)

Left: Safely parked on the main apron at McChord AFB, 52-0994 is at rest after the 2,350-mile (3,780km) flight from Selfridge AFB on October 9, 1986. (Doug Remington).

Below: 52-0994 was rescued from Willow Run Airport and flown to McChord AFB for display. The aircraft is seen at McChord being prepared for repainting in June 1987. (Raymond Rivard)

- 52-1000 was one of two C-124s retired to Aberdeen Proving Grounds, having been struck off charge at Tulsa Airport on May 22, 1972. The C-124s were parked on a remote range, but were largely undamaged as they had been used as storage sheds. However, in August 1982, Maj George Anderson and SMSgt Dave Florek from the 60th MAW wanted to exhibit a C-124 in the museum at Travis AFB, and the pair at Aberdeen were the only examples available. They visited Aberdeen, and despite years of neglect, the C-124 was in remarkably good condition. They decided that as the cost of shipping the C-124 by ground transportation was prohibitive, the most sensible (and fun) way to relocate to Travis was to fly the Globemaster!

Many former C-124 personnel volunteered their time and knowledge, and within a remarkably short period 52-1000 was ready. All four engines had to be replaced, and the damaged rudder was exchanged with the one from 51-0089, which was parked at Harlingen Airport. On November 15, 1983, the aircraft departed Phillips Army Airfield for the 50-mile (80km) flight to Dover AFB. Despite years of inactivity, everything worked remarkably well, with the C-124 settling onto the Dover runway with ease. Volunteers assembled at Dover to ensure that all mechanical systems were functioning correctly before the next stage in the journey, the 700-mile (1125km) flight to Dobbins AFB, which took place on November 18. There, members of the Georgia ANG's 116th TFW, who had previously flown Globemasters, performed the final restoration work and prepared the aircraft for the lengthy flight to Norton AFB for a short stopover, before the final delivery to Travis.

With all mechanical components overhauled, 52-1000 departed for Norton AFB, 2,140 miles (3443km) west. After a brief stop at the base, the C-124 completed the final leg of the journey on June 10, 1984,

Right: **After a great deal of hard work, volunteers finished repainting 52-0994 in similar markings to those applied when Globemasters were stationed at McChord AFB. (McChord AFB museum)**

Below: **Arriving at Dobbins AFB in November 1983, after the flight from Aberdeen Proving Grounds, is 52-1000 prior to receiving a major overhaul to enable the C-124 to fly across the US for one final time. (Ray Leader)**

Above: 52-1000 making a very low, fast flypast at Travis AFB to complete the delivery flight to the base Heritage Center on 10 June 1984. (USAF)

Left: The C-124C 52-1004 on display with the Pima County Air and Space Museum in 1973. (Ian Tate)

Below: The second-to-last C-124 to be retired to MASDC was Georgia ANG 52-1066, which arrived on September 19, 1974. Subsequently, the aircraft relocated to Wright-Patterson AFB for display. (Brian Rogers collection)

with a photo session above the Golden Gate Bridge, before landing at Travis AFB at exactly 14.00 that day. Once the engines were shut down for the final time, the crew officially transferred ownership to the Travis Heritage Center, where the aircraft resides to the present day as part of the Jimmy Doolittle Air and Space Museum. This was the first C-124 flight in nearly a decade.

- 52-1004 was retired for storage at MASDC on August 14, 1973, and was struck off charge on December 26 that year when relocated to the Pima Air and Space Museum adjacent to Davis-Monthan AFB.
- 52-1066 was flown to MASDC for storage on September 19, 1974, as the penultimate Globemaster to be retired – this and 53-0044 were flown to MASDC for storage the same day, but the latter was processed later, thereby becoming the final withdrawal. Being amongst the last pair, 52-1066 was selected to be displayed at the National Museum of the USAF at Wright-Patterson AFB. Following preparation by MASDC personnel, the aircraft was flown to Wright-Patterson during August 1975, and is displayed with serial number 51-0135.
- 52-1072 was struck off charge at Savannah on September 30, 1971, and relocated to the Air & Missile Museum at Florence Regional Airport, South Carolina. However, when the museum closed, the aircraft was relocated to Charleston AFB Heritage Park, and was displayed by 1986.
- 53-0050 was struck off charge at Salt Lake City, Utah, on June 13, 1972, and retired to the Aberdeen Providing Grounds. The aircraft was subsequently rescued and dismantled before being transported to Hill AFB for display at the Hill Aerospace Museum during 1992.

Right: Georgia ANG 52-1072 was SOC and transferred to the Air & Missile Museum at Florence, South Carolina, in September 1971. The aircraft was still at Florence in May 1984, although the museum closed shortly afterward, whereupon the airframe was reacquired by Charleston AFB for display in its Heritage Park. (Dave Wilton)

Below: Looking extremely forlorn after a lengthy period parked at the Aberdeen Proving Ground when seen during November 1986, 53-0050 was used for storage before being refurbished and relocated to Hill AFB for its Aerospace Museum. (Paul Bigelow)

One other C-124C that survived was 53-0044, which was sold to Surplus Aircraft Corporation in Tucson on June 4, 1976. The aircraft was subsequently bought by an un-named organization of South Valley View Boulevard in Las Vegas and registered as N3153F, and repainted in an attractive white and pale blue color scheme by MASDC staff. The C-124 was prepared for a single flight to McCarran Airport, Las Vegas, during November 1980, prior to being towed to an area on the corner of Koval Lane and Reno Avenue. Various roles were planned including a restaurant, night club, and an advertizing display. However, nothing came of these ideas, with the aircraft deteriorating, and eventually being cut up for scrap on March 26, 2001.

Beautifully restored C-124C 53-0050 wearing the markings of the 28th LSS, which was located at Hill AFB. It is on display at the base's aerospace museum during December 2004. (L Greenham)

Left: C-124C N3153F at Davis-Monthan AFB during November 1980, being prepared for a one-time flight to Las Vegas McCarran Airport for display. The aircraft was the subject of many projects, none of which came to fruition, with the aircraft being scrapped eventually. (Bon Knowles)

Below: Twenty years of exposure to the elements, and lacking any form of maintenance had taken their toll by the time the image was taken in November 1999. With no lucrative future, the aircraft was broken up for scrap 16 months later. (Stuart Prince)

Chapter 6

Globemaster Stories

Many of the personnel who flew or supported C-124 operations during the early period were World War Two veterans. As such, they were highly experienced at their tasks, with more than their fair share of "characters" within their ranks. Therefore, their yarns and anecdotes became the stuff of legend. While most stories had an element of truth, it is without doubt that these "Globemaster tales" were enhanced, depending upon the size of the crowd listening and the volume of alcohol being consumed!

The C-124 and the "Borrowed" Yak-23

During October 1953, intelligence agents from an undisclosed Balkan country approached the local Central Intelligence Agency (CIA) office offering to make a Soviet Yak-23 "Flora" jet fighter aircraft available to the US for a short period. Seemingly, the crated jet would be traveling through their country by railway to a second Balkan nation. The plan was for the first Balkan nation to "delay" the shipment, permitting the US to transport the fighter to the US, where it could quickly be assembled, inspected, and flown, before being repackaged. The crate would then continue it journey to the intended customer.

Called Project *Alpha*, the CIA contacted the Advanced Technical Intellicenge Center (ATIC) at Wright-Patterson AFB, which arranged for a C-124 of the 4th TCS, 62nd TCW, from Larson AFB to fly to Wright-Patterson and onto Westover AFB before continuing to a US base near Munich, West Germany. The pilot

Right: TAC C-124s did not display the command emblem until the latter period of their assignment. 51-0097 of the 4th TCS has the TAC badge on the tail when visiting Meacham Field, Fort Worth, Texas, during July 1956.

Below: TAC C-124A 51-0096 of the 4th TCS, 62nd TCW, shortly after delivery. (via Jerry Geer)

was Capt Leroy D Good, a highly experienced veteran of troop-carrier operations. Limited briefings were given, but did not include the destination or purpose of the mission. Capt Good was told that the final destination would be revealed once airborne. As it was impossible to conceal the large aircraft, the last leg of the journey was to be flown at night. Despite completing the majority of the inbound mission, Capt Good was ordered to return to Larson, with a second C-124 from his unit completing the pickup.

The second C-124 delivered its precious cargo to Wright-Patterson AFB, where ATIC personnel made the first Yak flight on November 4, 1953, and the last 21 days later. Capt Good was called upon to return the crate to the Balkans. His aircraft was 51-0097, which flew to Wright-Patterson, where personnel draped a black curtain across the cargo hold. Approximately a dozen men who spoke a foreign language also boarded the aircraft, along with a man wearing a USAF Colonel's uniform, but with no name tag. Again, the aircraft flew to the US base near Munich, where Good filed an instrument flight plan for an airfield north of the city. After take-off, the C-124 headed north, but almost immediately the colonel ordered Good to turn to a southerly course. The base air traffic control kept trying to contact the C-124 to query the flight plan deviation, but the Colonel ordered Good not to respond. When Good protested, he was told that the change had "all been arranged." More heading changes took place, before the C-124 was joined by an escort of two propeller-driven fighter aircraft. All three flew without lights switched on.

They landed in the middle of the night at a military airfield and were guided to a remote area. One of the Globemaster crew was handed a bottle of Serbian liqueur. Quickly, the cargo was unloaded, and the dozen foreign passengers departed. Soon afterwards, the Colonel instructed Good to fly to Paris Orly Airport, where he deplaned, before the C-124 flew back to Larson AFB.

Subsequently, it would appear that Capt Good had landed at an air base near Belgrade in (the former) Yugoslavia. Furthermore, the Yak-23 was being delivered to either Bulgaria or Romania. A possible explanation for the actions of the Yugoslav government was that President Tito wished to foster better relations with Western nations, and what better means than with an intelligence gift. And the C-124 was center stage in this espionage performance!

Area 51

The C-124 performed many other clandestine missions, with the delivery of the ultra secret Lockheed U-2 being one of the most fascinating. On July 24, 1955, a C-124 transported the first Lockheed U-2 from Burbank Airport to Groom Lake, Nevada. The dismantled U-2 was covered in shrouds to

1st SSS C-124C 52-1018 ferrying Lockheed U-2 components from Burbank Airport to Groom Lake, Nevada, during the second half of the 1950s. (Lockheed)

conceal the highly classified reconnaissance aircraft. The C-124 was positioned in a remote area of Burbank, close to the legendary Skunk Works, where the U-2 was developed and built. The aircrew was not told anything about its cargo, or about the destination, but were provided with approximate details of the return distance required. This information was necessary so the crew could estimate fuel requirements. With the precious cargo successfully loaded, the C-124 departed Burbank and headed northeast for the 350-mile (563km) flight to the desolate airstrip deep in the Nevada desert. The aircrew was told only the headings and approximate distance to fly. Once within close proximity of the airstrip, the runway lights were switched on, enabling the startled flight deck crew to land. As soon as the Globemaster touched down, the runway lights were switched off. A "follow me" vehicle guided the C-124 to a parking area, where the U-2 was unloaded by Lockheed technicians. The C-124 was then cleared to depart, with the runway lighting being switched on again for the duration of the time the aircraft required to take off. Once airborne, the airstrip returned to its nocturnal desolation.

With a maximum take-off weight of 216,000lb (97 tonnes), the C-124 was requested to land on the baked lakebed to avoid wear and tear to Groom Lake's paved, thin runway. However, on the day of the first U-2 delivery, rain had softened the lakebed surface, and the base Commander, Col Richard Newton, refused to allow the C-124 to land on the asphalt strip. He relented after Skunk Works' chief Kelly Johnson expressed his dissatisfaction and called CIA headquarters. Two hours later, using reverse-propeller-pitch for braking, the C-124 landed on partially deflated tires. After the dust cleared, the Commander noted that the runway had a quarter-inch indentation running a distance of 50ft. "It was really gory for a first meeting with Newton," Johnson later wrote in his personal log. Article 341, as the U-2 was known, was unloaded and the C-124 departed.

Some delivery flights were conducted by SAC, while others were flown by MATS. Eventually, flights landed at Groom Lake in daylight. Other C-124 sorties were used to transport CIA U-2s from Groom Lake to various operating locations in England, West Germany, Turkey, and Pakistan. The U-2 remained in operational service after the C-124 was retired, with the Lockheed C-141 Starlifter being used occasionally, although increasingly the U-2 has flown directly to overseas destinations.

Broken Arrow Nuclear Weapons Loss

Accidents and losses of nuclear weapons have happened on at least 30 occasions, despite stringent arrangements being in place to minimize such occurrences. Several code names were in place to alert senior military personnel and government officials to the type of situation. Broken Arrow was best known, and was termed as an accidental event involving nuclear weapons, warheads or components, which would not create the risk of nuclear war. Many such incidents entailed USAF aircraft being involved in crashes or emergency circumstances. Some of these incidents involved nuclear weapons being carried aboard bombers, such as the Boeing B-47 Stratojet and Boeing B-52 Stratofortress. However, at least three incidents involved the C-124.

On July 28, 1957, a C-124 departed Dover AFB for Europe. The cargo was three plutonium warheads and a nuclear capsule, although all were inert with no nuclear components installed. Soon after take-off, the aircraft experienced problems with engines number one and two. The pilot declared an emergency, and applied full power to the two remaining engines, as well as a great deal of rudder and stick to counter the adverse yaw. Despite the pilot inputs, the aircraft continued to lose altitude, and at 2,500ft (762m), the decision was made to jettison one of the weapons. A second followed soon afterwards. Both weapons sank to the bottom of the ocean, although no detonation was observed. The C-124 diverted to Atlantic City, New Jersey. The US government immediately instigated a search for the two weapons, but no trace was found. They are believed to be deep in ocean off the New Jersey/Delaware coast.

Left: 1607th ATW C-124C 52-1008 at Dover AFB in August 1959. An aircraft similar to this one was involved in the "Broken Arrow" incident on July 28, 1957. (Steve Miller)

Below: MATS Atlantic Division C-124C 53-0010 at Rickenbacker AFB, Ohio, in May 1956, operated by the 1st ATS at Dover AFB. (Bob Garrard)

C-124A 49-0254 of the 3rd SSS crashed on take-off at Barksdale AFB on July 6, 1959, with the blazing aircraft coming to rest one mile from the runway end. Nuclear weapons were aboard, one of which was destroyed and others damaged in the fire. Minor radiation was leaked, but insufficient to cause an emergency.

The third incident occurred on October 11, 1965, when 63rd TCW C-124C 53-0010 caught fire on the ramp at Wright-Patterson AFB while being refuelled. The cargo was nuclear weapon components and dummy training devices. The fire consumed the fuselage. The nuclear devices were damaged, with minor radiation contamination locally.

Delivering Warheads – A Close Encounter

An important mission that was flown on a "war time" footing was the resupply of US missile sites overseas. 1st Lt Dewitt Swanson recalls his first such mission, flying a C-124 from Dover AFB to Long Beach in July 1961 to collect 13 nuclear warheads for delivery to Turkey. The missiles were not armed, so there was no danger of a nuclear explosion, but they could release a radioactive cloud if ruptured, so there was a high level of stress for the crew. After securing the warheads aboard, the C-124 flew to Tinker AFB to refuel before continuing onto Ankara, Turkey. "After refueling, we did our pre-flight engine runs before beginning the take-off roll. The aircraft was at maximum weight with full fuel tanks."

After lift-off, the undercarriage was raised to reduce drag, and the aircraft levelled off at 250ft (76m) to build up speed. Almost immediately, there was a loud explosion and the airplane did a severe yaw to the left. The engineer at the control panel was Senior Master Sgt Dale Sapp, who announced that we had lost the left inboard engine:

Right: MAC C-124C 51-5192 departing Hickam AFB during 1967. Several years earlier, at this stage in the flight, a Dover-based C-124 lost an engine when it exploded, followed by the remaining three shutting down due to contaminated fuel. (Nick Williams)

Below: 52-1045 of the 436th MAW deployment to Rhein-Main, at Mildenhall, May 1968. (R A Schofield)

I told him to shut it down and to leave max power on the other engines. His reply was, 'Swanny, you didn't understand, I mean we lost the engine, there is nothing there anymore!' My reply was to say 'ok shut everything you can down and send the second flight engineer back to the cargo hold to give us an eyeball.' About that time, the other flight engineer yelled over the intercom that there was nothing left of that engine other than a black indentation in the wing and there were a few holes in the fuselage and scattered around parts of the engine scattered around. So, we declared an emergency and started a shallow turn to land at Tinker; although midway through the turn the left outboard engine quit. It won't run and now we have a big problem because it is difficult to control a fully loaded C-124 with two engines out on one side. I decided we wouldn't make the active runway and elected to attempt a landing on the cross runway, it wasn't as long but that was the least of my concerns. Just as we turn final at about 200ft [61m], the right inboard engine caught fire. It was still running and I told Sapp to leave it running and shut it down immediately over the end of the runway, if it was still running. In the meantime, the co-pilot had alerted the tower that we had 'hot' cargo, which meant nuclear weapons on board. During all this I had the navigators and the second engineer go below the flight deck to hand crank the landing gear down if we needed to. One of the navigators bitched about it saying that would be the worst place to be if we crashed; I informed him, if we crashed, there would be no safe place on the airplane, so he did it. Fortunately, we didn't need to manually lower the gear down, there was enough hydraulic pressure being supplied by the running engines, and the gear or the hydraulic hoses hadn't been damaged. Over the end of the runway Sapp shut down the burning engine and had no sooner done so when the last engine quit. Well, it wasn't the best or prettiest landing I ever made but we were all satisfied with it. This was a well trained crew that knew their jobs and did them well, which resulted in an airplane and a valuable cargo being saved. One thing I didn't notice until we deplaned was so many emergency vehicles in one spot in my life!

The cause of the problem was contaminated fuel. A replacement C-124 arrived later from Dover AFB and another crew completed the task.

"Zero Zero" by Charles Svoboda

It happened sometime in 1965, in Germany. I was a co-pilot, so I knew, everything there was to know about flying, and I was frustrated by pilots like my aircraft commander. He was one of those by-the-numbers types, no class, no imagination, and no 'feel' for flying. You have to be able to feel an airplane. So what if your altitude is a little off, or if the glide slope indicator is off a hair? If it feels okay then it is okay. That's what I believed.

Every time he let me make an approach, even in VFR (Visual Flight Rules) conditions, he demanded perfection. Not the slightest deviation was permitted. 'If you can't do it when there is no pressure, you surely can't do it when the pucker factor increases,' he would say. When he shot an approach, it was as if all the instruments were frozen – perfection, but no class.

Then came a routine flight from the Azores to Germany. The weather was okay; we had 45,000lb [20.4 tonnes] of fuel and enough cargo to bring the weight of our C-124 Globemaster up to 180,000lb [81.6 tonnes], 5,000lb [2.2 tonnes] below the maximum allowable. It would be an easy, routine flight all the way.

Halfway to the European mainland, the weather started getting bad. I kept getting updates by high-frequency radio. Our destination, a fighter base, went zero/zero (visibility). Our two alternates followed shortly thereafter. All of France was down. We held for two hours, and the weather got worse. Somewhere I heard a fighter pilot declare an emergency because of minimum fuel. He shot two approaches and saw nothing. On the third try, he flamed out and had to eject. We made a precision radar approach; there was nothing but fuzzy fog at minimums. The sun was setting. Now I started to sweat a little. I turned on the instrument lights. When I looked out to where the wings should be, I couldn't even see the navigation lights 85ft [25m] from my eyes. I could barely make out a dull glow from the exhaust stacks of the closest engine, and then only on climb power.

When we reduced power to maximum endurance, that friendly glow faded. The pilot asked the engineer where we stood on fuel. The reply was, 'I don't know – we're so low that the book says the gauges are unreliable below this point.' The navigator became a little frantic. We didn't carry parachutes on regular MATS flights, so we couldn't follow the fighter pilot's example. We would land or crash with the airplane.

The pilot then asked me which of the two nearby fighter bases had the widest runway. I looked it up and we declared an emergency as we headed for that field. The pilot then began his briefing. 'This will be for real. No missed approach. We'll make an ILS [instrument landing system] and get precision radar to keep us honest. Co-pilot, we'll use half flaps. That'll put the approach speed a little higher, but the pitch angle will be almost level, requiring less altitude change in the flare.' Why hadn't I thought of that? Where was my 'feel' and 'class' now? The briefing continued, 'I'll lock on

52-0956 at Rhein Main, circa 1961. Charles Svoboda recalls a flight from the Azores to Germany that culminated in a zero-visibility landing. (Ralf Manteufel)

A fine study of C-124C 52-1035 of the 1501st ATW near Travis AFB. (Douglas)

the gauges. You get ready to take over and complete the landing if you see the runway – that way there will be less room for trouble with me trying to transition from instruments to visual with only a second or two before touchdown.' Hey, he's even going to take advantage of his co-pilot, I thought. He's not so stupid, after all. 'Until we get the runway, you call off every 100ft [30.5m] above touchdown; until we get down to 100ft, use the pressure altimeter. Then switch to the radar altimeter for the last 100 ft, and call off every 25ft [7.6m]. Keep me honest on the airspeed, also. Engineer, when we touchdown, I'll cut the mixtures with the master control lever, and you cut all of the mags (magnetos). Are there any questions? Let's go!'

All of a sudden, this unfeeling, by-the-numbers robot was making a lot of sense. Maybe he really was a pilot and maybe I had something more to learn about flying. We made a short procedure turn to save gas. Radar helped us to get to the outer marker. Half a mile away, we performed the Before Landing Checklist; gear down, flaps 20 degrees. The course deviation indicator was locked in the middle, with the glide slope indicator beginning its trip down from the top of the case. When the GSI centred, the pilot called for a small power reduction, lowered the nose slightly, and all of the instruments, except the altimeter, froze.

My Lord, that man had a feel for that airplane! He thought something, and the airplane, all 135,000lb [61 tonnes] of it, did what he thought. '500ft,' I called out, '400ft……..300ft……200ft, MATS minimums…….100ft, Air Force minimums; I'm switching to the radar altimeter ……..75ft nothing in sight……50ft, still nothing….25ft, airspeed 100 knots.' The nose of the aircraft rotated just a couple of degrees, and the airspeed started down. The pilot then casually said, 'Hang on, we're landing.' 'Airspeed 90 knots….10ft, here we go!' The pilot reached up and cut the mixtures with the master control lever, without taking his eyes off the instruments. He told the engineer to cut all the mags to reduce the chance of fire. CONTACT! I could barely feel it. As smooth a landing as I have ever known, and I couldn't even tell if we were on the runway, because we could only see the occasional blur of a light streaking by. 'Co-pilot, verify hydraulic boost is on, I'll need it for brakes and steering.' I complied. 'Hydraulic boost pump is on, pressure is up.' The brakes came on slowly— we didn't want to skid this big beast now. I looked over at the pilot. He was still on the instruments, steering to keep the course deviation indicator in the center, and that is exactly where it stayed. 'Airspeed, 50 knots.' We might make it yet. 'Airspeed, 25 knots.' We'll make it if we don't run off a cliff. Then I heard a strange sound. I could hear the whir of the gyros, the buzz of the inverters, and a low frequency thumping. Nothing else. The thumping was my pulse, and I couldn't hear anyone breathing. We had made it! We were standing still!

The aircraft commander was still all pilot. 'After-landing checklist, get all those motors, radar and un-necessary radios off while we still have batteries. Co-pilot, tell them that we have arrived, to send a Follow-Me truck out to the runway because we can't even see the edges.' I left the VHF on and thanked GCA for the approach. The guys in the tower didn't believe we were there. They had walked outside and couldn't hear or see anything. We assured them that we were there, somewhere on the localizer centerline, with about half a mile showing on the DME. We waited about 20 minutes for the truck. Not being in our customary hurry, just getting our breath back and letting our pulses diminish to a reasonable rate.

Then I felt it. The cockpit shuddered as if the nose gear had run over a bump. I told the loadmaster to go out the crew entrance to see what happened. He dropped the door (which is immediately in front of the nose gear), and it hit something with a loud, metallic bang. He came on the interphone and said 'Sir, you'll never believe this. The Follow-Me truck couldn't see us and ran smack into our nose tire with his bumper, but he bounced off, and nothing is hurt.' The pilot then told the tower that we were parking the bird right where it was and that we would come in via the truck. It took a few minutes to get our clothing and to button up the airplane. I climbed out and saw the nose tires straddling the runway centreline. A few feet away were the truck with its embarrassed driver.

Total damage – one dent in the hood of the Follow-Me truck where the hatch had opened onto it. Then I remembered the story from *Fate Is The Hunter*. When Gann was an airline co-pilot making a simple night-range approach, his captain kept lighting matches in front of his eyes. It scared and infuriated Gann. When they landed, the captain said that Gann was ready to upgrade to captain. If he could handle a night-range approach with all of that harassment, then he could handle anything.

At last I understood what true professionalism is. Being a pilot isn't all seat-of-the-pants flying and glory. It's discipline, practice, study, analysis and preparation. It's precision. If you can't keep the gauges where you want them with everything free and easy, how can you keep them there when everything goes wrong?

C-124 Humour

There's a story about a C-124 and a McDonnell F-4 Phantom jet fighter on intersecting taxiways at Rhein-Main AB. The F-4 pilot asked air traffic control what the Globemaster's intentions were. It is said that the C-124 pilot opened the clam shell doors in the nose and announced, "I'm going to eat you."

Above: 436th MAW C-124C 52-0950 taxiing at Rhein-Main AB in May 1968 with the flight engineer atop the open hatchway to guide the pilot from this lofty position. The extra pair of eyes was vital, as the cockpit was positioned ahead of the nose wheel. (Lindsay Peacock)

Right: 349th MAW C-124C 51-0115 taxies past 436th MAW 52-1007 at Rhein-Main during January 1969. For decades, Rhein-Main was the primary gateway to the huge US military garrison in Germany, with daily C-124 flights arriving from the US with supplies. (Lindsay Peacock)

Air Transport Nuclear Navigators

USAF Navigator Observer Association Historian Ronald P Barrett recalls some of his experiences as a nuclear navigator flying C-124s worldwide.

For the majority of the C-124's active duty career, one of the most important tasks was the delivery of nuclear weapons and their components. Understandably aircrew positions for aircraft associated with the task were considered the best of the best. One of the positions was that of nuclear navigator, known simply as 'nuclear navs.'

The first nuclear navs were those who crewed the B-29s of the 509th Composite Group, which delivered the two atomic bombs over Japan in August 1945. As the post of navigator gained prominence, and nuclear weapons proliferated, so the need for specialist nuclear nav expanded. Within the transport community, the C-54 was the first aircraft that delivered anything and everything related to the new 'special weapons.' However, the C-124 was far more capable, with its substantial cargo hold designed specifically to accommodate such weapons. Personnel assigned to the three LSSs included nuclear navs, who were expected to fly long distances using only basic navigational aids, and with the smallest of fuel reserves. During trans-Pacific sorties, for example, they routinely encountered adverse climatic conditions such as freak winds, thunderstorms due to the inter-tropical-convergence zone weather, as well as the constant engine problems of the old radial powerplants fitted to the C-54 and C-124. Neither was pressurized, with the operating altitude ordinarily around 10,000ft (3,054m), which made for a bumpy ride for all on board. All passengers and crew had to endure a ten-hour plus flight, with no air conditioning, little cabin ventilation, a very rudimentary toilet, and troop seating alongside the cargo.

President Eisenhower, following President Truman's lead, approved of higher special weapons production rates. Secretary of State John Foster Dulles announced that henceforth the nuclear doctrine of the US would be that of, 'massive retaliation.' The increase in the number of weapons led to the creation of the three LSSs mentioned earlier. AFLC was responsible for USAF's operational special weapons, to support both the Atomic Energy Commission (AEC) and the DoD, traveling

Left: A rare shot of AFLC 52-1006 of the 28th LSS landing at Tachikawa AB in September 1962. (Geta-O)

Below: 52-1013 wearing the 19th ATS (Special) emblem on the tail, as part of the 62nd TCW stationed at Kelly AFB. The primary duty was transportation of special weapons and their components, and this aircraft is seen at RAF Greenham Common late in 1963. (via APN)

worldwide between the military bases and the Operational Storage Sites (OSS). Additional duties included ferrying weapons between the AEC production facilities, and the research test sites at Johnson Island and Kwajalein.

The peak year for production was 1962 under President Kennedy, when the US was building one nuclear weapon a day! There were more than 10,000 nuclear warheads and bombs in the US military forces. The logistics and maintenance of this ever-increasing nuclear stockpile required a significant element of air transport support. During the first half of the 1950s an atmospheric nuclear test was being carried out almost every month, with the C-124 at the forefront of weapons delivery.

The standard nuclear air transport C-124 crew was two pilots, one navigator, two flight engineers, one loadmaster and often a flight mechanic. On special, special loads we also had security guards and additional scientific personnel flying along with us. Two-man concept clearances were required to be physically around the nuclear weapons and components at all times. Later, a system known as Permissive Access Links-Lock (PAL) was introduced to safeguard security of nuclear weapons. All crewmembers were Top Secret and 'two man reliability concept' cleared. Navigators were crypto trained and both the navs and pilots were courier-duty cleared.

However, as nuclear weapons became smaller, and procedures well developed, handling became simpler. Furthermore the C-141 began replacing the C-124 in the role. By this time, the LSS units had changed designation to ATS (Special), and eventually normal MASs. Whereas the C-124 often required an internal overhead crane on rails to move these weapons, eventually movement by the C-141 was simplified with the smaller weapons using palletized loading systems. Military Airlift Command assigned the term Primary Nuclear Mission to the task.

The usual mission profile was to do a classified pre-brief the day prior to launch of the sortie. Missions were for the ease of it, called 'West' or 'East' just to give general direction as all else was classified. Missions were from a few days to weeks in length. A mission lasting one month was a really long one. No matter the maximum time on duty, the time off between missions was 72 hours. Because the C-124s were getting in to their final days, most missions had break-down delays. On one mission, the 7th LSS had a serious refueling fire, on the hot spot, at Wright-Patterson AFB, Ohio. It destroyed the C-124 and the nuclear goodies inside! Oh my! Lucky though, the aircraft commander was the Squadron Commander. So none of us Lieutenants took any heat for the resultant Broken Arrow (the name that was given when a nuke load was involved in an accident). On another we took a small arms round through the wing forward spar (the wing was a wet wing), and it poured aviation gasoline down the crawl way, which gathered in puddles in the lower bay! Lucky, no fire, because we were full of flares! My last year of flying in the 7th Log was very eventful as every-other flight was terminated as an in-flight emergency. At the end of our missions, a debrief was conducted and nav logs filed. Needless to say, we flew to all kinds of bases, and all over the world, meeting Cold War demands as they came up. Just now some of the missions are

52-1061 of the 1607th ATW is about to unload a Thor missile in the UK, circa 1960. Transporting these missiles to the UK was believed to have been a specialist task assigned to the 1607th. (Douglas)

being declassified like *Pot Pie I* and *Pot Pie II,* which were the warhead retrieval missions, from Europe after Kennedy said, the Russians blinked during the Cuban Missile Crisis. I can tell you the Russians may have blinked, and while their eyes were closed we rushed to remove many warheads from Europe! [Operation *Pot Pie* was the removal of the US Jupiter missiles from Turkey and Italy after the Cuban Missile Crisis.]

I loved navigating the C-124 because it had all of the aids that allowed me to be a true navigator and to use celestial-sextants, pressure pattern-geotropic wind computations, ground speed by timing, radio fixing, PIREP weather watch, and interpret Loran sky and ground waves. And now there are no navigators, or very few, to say the least, as they have been replaced by the more reliable GPS system. It was a great and important mission. And the USAF has no history of the ATS(S)s or LSS squadrons.

MSgt James M Zeitler (Ret) and the C-124

I enlisted in August 1963, with Dover being my first assignment. Stationed there were C-124s, C-97s, C-133s, F-105s I believe, but I didn't work on anything but heavies. When I was scheduled to ship out to Lajes Field we received the first C-141. I was on a return flight from Hickam AFB where we were supporting the airlift to Vietnam. We had 100 maintenance folks on board and were due to land at Carswell AFB in Texas. We had been circling for quite some time when the flight engineer came down to the cargo floor and said '[the] pilot sure would like to have a word with you.' I went to the cockpit and the pilot advises me the left main gear won't come out of the wheel well. Can I do anything about it? It seems they were getting ready to foam the runway. I told him yes. I had seen my toolbox in the back of the aircraft, and I needed a couple of long cargo straps and three or four big guys. He asked what the straps were for, and I told him I was going to tie one end of them around my waist and I wanted the four guys to make sure the other end remained inside the aircraft.

I crawled out through the wing and got behind #2 engine, wrapped my legs around a spar that came from the wing spar to the back of the engine. I used a large screwdriver to pry the uplock over centre, and the gear lowered to the down and locked position. I immediately puked all over Carswell AFB. All I could see below us was emergency vehicle lights everywhere. The pilot took me to the O-Club and bought me a steak dinner and many cold 'beverages.' I loved the C-124 and the C-133. Good aircraft.

MSgt Zeitler was literally hanging onto the wing spar, with nothing between himself and the earth below. Indeed, it was not uncommon for flight engineers to remain in the wing, once a stuck main undercarriage was manually lowered. On several occasions, these brave crew members crawled from inside the wing after the aircraft was safely on the ground and stopped!

Almost every member of the C-124 flying community has a story to tell of how the robust and resilient Globemaster overcame technical issues, due in no small part to the fortitude of the crew.

C-124C 49-0255 of the 916th MAG at Carswell AFB departing Hickam AFB on a resupply flight to SEA during 1968. Note the inscription "100,000" on the clam shell doors – almost certainly indicating the number of miles flown since joining the unit in April 1965. (Nick Williams)

Chapter 7

Color Schemes and Markings

The Globemaster straddled the evolutionary period when USAF aircraft transitioned from all-over natural metal finish, with a minimum of unit identity, through to a high-visibility era bedecked with Arctic Red or Day-Glo orange, before adopting schemes comparable with the airliners of the period. The initial markings applied varied between Command assignments, although the wholesale transfer of almost every C-124 to MATS saw a more unified set of markings. Several Commands added Arctic Red to the tail of each aircraft due to regular resupply missions to northern latitudes such as Greenland.

Alaskan Air Command: Due to operations taking place primarily within Alaska, the tail and outer wings tips were painted Arctic Red to aid recognition. Apart from the command and wing emblem, no additional markings were applied.

AMC/AFLC: The Command's aircraft were, like all other operators, initially natural metal finish. An individual scheme was later adopted, with a white upper surface beginning aft of the cockpit, with the lower surface retaining the natural metal finish. A large squadron emblem was displayed to the nose, and Arctic Red was applied to the tail and rear fuselage. Later, the red area was removed, and replaced by Day-Glo orange in a similar fashion to MATS. The 3079th ADW emblem was positioned on the tail. AMC and later AFLC titles were applied along the upper fuselage.

The period of assignment to Alaskan Air Command was brief but required the 17th TAS to apply Arctic Red to the tail as well as the Command emblem. 51-0098 was one of the first two to join the 17th TAS in December 1969, remaining assigned until retired to MASDC during February 1972, where the aircraft is seen during October 1973.

Above: Shortly after acquiring 50-0105, the 937th TCG at Tinker AFB applied "Wings of OK. C." on the nose in recognition of the unit being stationed in the suburbs of Oklahoma City. (Doug Slowiak collection)

Left: 51-0181 of the 901st MAG at Hanscom AFB unloading cargo through the center fuselage hatchway. To ensure the center of gravity was maintained during loading and unloading, the tail stand was positioned to prevent the rear tipping up.

CONAC/AFRES/ANG: The reserve aircraft displayed almost the same markings as MATS and MAC, to simplify incorporating into the active duty when mobilized. CONAC aircraft displayed the MATS-style tail stripe, but with the broad yellow section replaced with white containing the letters "CAC." When CONAC was replaced by AFRES, these letters were presented within the stripe.

The ANG aircraft, on the other hand, were divided between those that adopted MAC style of markings, but with ANG presented in the tail band, while others had the appropriate state painted along the upper fuselage. The state name was also reproduced on the rear fuselage along with the ANG emblem. The numbered Group or Wing was presented on the nose wheel door. Surprisingly, art was rare, although one C-124 displayed a cartoon of Andy Capp on the nose. Additionally, an AFRES C-124 had "1,000,000 miles" painted on the nose during the late 1960s.

MAC: When MAC replaced MATS in January 1966, the new Command retained the markings of the latter. The yellow and dark blue tail band containing MATS was replaced with MAC. The Command emblem was almost identical to that of MATS and was therefore also retained.

MATS: MATS aircraft also featured natural metal finish, but within a very short time the Service had adopted more attractive markings. The nose carried the Service emblem flanked by a yellow rectangular

Above left: C-124s rarely had any form of art applied, but Tennessee ANG C-124C 52-1034 was decorated with the cartoon figure Andy Capp on the nose, when seen at Yokota AB in June 1972.

Above right: 53-0034 of the 61st MAW at Richmond Airport, Virginia, during November 1966. Note the black and white colors on the nose wheel door. (Ben Dannecker)

During the MATS and early MAC era, C-124s were almost daily visitors to Prestwick Airport. 436th MAW 52-0952 braves the elements during March 1967. (Eric Roscoe)

design outlined in dark blue. The familiar "MATS tail stripe" consisting of thick dark blue band outlined in yellow carried the relevant Division. When the three Divisions were replaced by Eastern and Pacific Transport Air Forces on July 1, 1958, the tail stripe contained just "MATS." Some aircraft had an Arctic Red tail. Later in the 1950s, the Service adopted an airline style of color scheme. The natural metal scheme was retained on the lower section of the fuselage, while the upper sector was painted white. Bisecting the two sections was a dark blue cheatline. The nose and rear fuselage were marked with a Day-Glo orange stripe – this additional color had largely been removed by 1963. The all-silver scheme remained throughout. The Wing or Group identity was presented on the nose wheel door.

PACAF: The aircraft were operated briefly, and were flown in natural metal finish, with a white area aft of the cockpit. No Command or unit insignia were added.

53-0006 was inscribed "D.D. Johnston, Norwalk – LA Beach City School District." This was in reference to a mid-air collision on February 1, 1958, between a USAF C-118A and a US Navy Lockheed P2V-5F Neptune, which occurred above a school, and claimed the lives of 48 people, including one on the ground. The aircraft is seen taxiing at Prestwick Airport in June 1959. (McIntyre collection)

C-124 at Bovingdon in May 1962, transporting John Glenn's Gemini spacecraft *Friendship 7* on a world tour. Glenn was the first American to orbit the Earth. 53-0009 was especially inscribed for the tour and was operated by the 1607th ATW at Dover AFB at the time.

SAC received the first operational C-124As to be delivered, and added the C-124C in 1953. 52-0974 joined the 4th SSS at Ellsworth AFB and remained with the unit until January 1961. (via Terry Panopalis)

SAC: SAC was the first C-124 operator. The aircraft retained the natural metal finish, but with individual squadron colors applied to each side of the forward fuselage. Arctic Red was soon added to the extreme rear fuselage and outer wings. The first three SAC squadrons also had a cheatline of the squadron colors. A fourth squadron was added, but lacked these insignia. Before the middle of the decade, the individual squadron markings were removed. Later in the decade, the star-spangled blue Command sash was applied to the rear fuselage. As aircraft underwent major overhaul, the markings began to vary, with some retaining the Arctic colors, while others lacked this scheme.

TAC: Similar to SAC, TAC aircraft had colorful markings applied to the nose and forward fuselage to signify the Wing. The 63rd TCG/TCW featured the squadron emblem ahead of stylized wings, or other similarly shaped decoration. Those of the 62nd TCG/TCW had two horizontal bands positioned across the nose and extending below the cockpit before joining together and ending in a point. In both cases, the style of the markings differentiated between the two wings, while the different colors, almost certainly indicated the relevant squadron. Additionally, "United States Air Force" was painted on the forward fuselage, and eventually the legend "Troop Carrier" was added. A large rectangular Arctic Red section was applied to the tail, and the extreme rear fuselage. This latter pattern was only displayed for a limited period. Others received a white scheme to the upper forward fuselage almost as far as the wingroot - this being to reflect heat from the cockpit area. Some had a thick cheatline. When the TAC TCSs joined MATS, they adopted the standard scheme of the latter Service. It would appear there was no definitive pattern to the TAC aircraft; changes happened often, and were applied when aircraft were cycled through major overhaul.

Right: **52-1014 wearing the nose markings applied to 62nd TCW aircraft, but lacking the squadron badge. The aircraft is supporting the Idaho ANG deploy away from Boise Air Terminal during August 1956. (Sterling E Weaver)**

Below: **This aircraft displays a mix of markings consisting of the 53rd TCS emblem and nose markings of TAC, along with the MATS tail stripe containing the legend "Continental," for the Division responsible for the parent 63rd TCW at Donaldson AFB. The image was taken shortly after the transition period from TAC to MATS in July 1957.**

Representative Markings on 49-0258

Presented below are a superb set of drawings depicting 49-0258 during different periods of its 18 years in operational service. The Arctic Red areas were applied due to many operations to remote regions in the northern hemisphere. In the event of an aircraft making an emergency landing, the red paint would aid rescue efforts.

The drawings were kindly supplied by the AMC Museum at Dover AFB.

3rd SSS, SAC, Hunter AFB, 1951

3rd SSS, SAC, Hunter AFB, 1952

3rd SSS, SAC, Barksdale AFB, 1954 (appeared in movie *Strategic Air Command*)

3rd SSS, SAC, Barksdale AFB, 1959

305th TCS, mobilized for TAC, Tinker AFB, 1961

1503rd ATW, MATS, Tachikawa AFB, Japan, 1963

916th TCG, AFRES, Carswell AFB, 1967

MATS markings, AMC Museum, 2007

It is worth presenting the history of 49-0258, as this helps explain the evolution of the color schemes. Note the 1961 design has the basic MATS pattern, but with TAC in the tail band and its emblem on the rear fuselage. This is because TAC was still the gaining command when the reserve unit was mobilized for active duty. The gaining command status for the CONAC Squadrons was hereditary and had not been changed when TAC relinquished its C-124s to MATS in 1957.

History of AMC Museum's C-124A 49-0258

January 31, 1951	Delivered to the USAF
February 1951	3rd SSS Hunter AFB
January 1952	3rd SSS moved to Barksdale AFB
Summer 1954	Appeared in movie *Strategic Air Command*
April 1961	Reassigned to 305th TCS (CONAC), Tinker AFB
October 1961	Squadron mobilized to active duty with TAC
March 1962	Assigned to active duty with 442nd TCW, Tinker AFB
July 1962	Reassigned to 1502nd ATW (MATS), Hickam AFB
March 1963	Transferred to 1503rd ATW (MATS), Tachikawa AB
July 1964	Returned to 1502nd ATW (MATS), Hickam AFB
August 1965	Transferred to 916th TCG (CONAC), Carswell AFB
January 1966	Unit redesignated 916th MAG (CONAC)
August 1968	Reassigned from CONAC to AFRES
July 1969	Dropped from the inventory, and transferred to the 3902nd ABW Offutt AFB and for display with the SAC Museum
1969 to 1998	On display at SAC Museum, Offutt AFB
1998	SAC Museum closed and relocated. 49-0258 left behind at Offutt AFB
2002 to 2004	Disassembled and transferred to AMC Museum, Dover AFB, for restoration and display
2005 to 2006	Reassembly and restoration in museum hangar
2006	Restoration completed, and displayed outside.

49-0258 being relocated to a hanger at Dover AFB after dismantled sections had been flown in by C-5s from Offutt AFB during 2004. Whereas other C-124s had been made airworthy for their one-time flight to a museum, 49-0258 had spent 30 years enduring the Nebraska elements and would have required a prohibitive amount of restorative maintenance. (AMC Museum)

Life History of 52-0994, 53-0050 and 53-0052

The life history of three C-124Cs is presented below to detail the varied unit assignments of these aircraft.

52-0994 followed a familiar career, initially with the active duty, before Air National Guard service.

October 5, 1953	Delivered to 3rd ATS, 1700th ATG, Brookley AFB
June 1958	Relocated to 3rd ATS, 1608th ATW, Charleston AFB
March 1962	Reassigned to 1607th ATW, Dover AFB
August 1965	Transferred to 63rd TCW, Hunter AFB
January 1966	Redesignated 63rd MAW
January 1967	Reassigned to 116th MAG, Georgia ANG, Dobbins AFB
December 1972	Transferred to 165th MAG, Georgia ANG, Savannah MAP
December 1972	Dropped from the inventory, and transferred to the Detroit Institute of Aeronautics
October 8, 1986	Loaned by the National Museum of the Air Force to the McChord Air Museum

53-0050 was the third from last C-124 to be produced, and enjoyed an average history, prior to becoming one of just nine survivors to be displayed. The purchase cost was $1,646,000, with delivery taking place from the Douglas plant at Long Beach on May 4, 1955.

May 4, 1955	Delivered to 15th ATS, 1607th ATW (MATS), Dover AFB
June 1965	Reassigned to 28th ATS (Special), 1501st ATW, Hill AFB
August 1965	Transferred to 62nd ATW, McChord AFB
November 1969	Reassigned to 151st MAG, Utah ANG, Salt Lake City Airport
June 1972	Transferred to the US Army at the Aberdeen Proving Ground storage facility. Was scheduled to be used for ballistic research
1992	Acquired by the Hill Aerospace Museum for static display
	Subsequently restored by museum volunteers and members of the 28th LSS/MAS Historical Association.

53-0052 was the last C-124 produced, spending its entire 14 years assigned to various MATS/MAC units. The vast majority of the period was at bases in the Western US and Pacific region, apart from a brief spell on the East Coast. Surprisingly, there was no reservist assignment.

May 2, 1955	Accepted by USAF at Long Beach
June 6, 1955	Delivered to 1501st ATW, Travis AFB
December 1956	Transferred to 1502nd ATW, Hickam AFB
June 1957	Transferred back to 1501st ATW, Travis AFB
June 1959	Relocated to 1608th AW, Charleston AFB

The final C-124 produced was 53-0052, which was flown solely by MATS and MAC. It is seen here receiving engine maintenance at RAF Mildenhall during August 1964. (Peter Cooper)

June 1960	Transferred to 63rd TCW, Donaldson AFB
November 1962	Participated in the last C-124 Operation *Deep Freeze* season
December 1963	Moved to Hunter AFB with 63rd TCW
June 1965	Transferred to 62nd ATW, McChord AFB
January 1966	Redesignated to 62nd MAW, McChord AFB
April 1967	Transferred to 443rd MAW, Tinker AFB
June 1967	Reassigned back to 62nd MAW, McChord AFB
November 22, 1969	Retired to MASDC at Davis-Monthan AFB
January 1970	Struck off charge, and scrapped soon afterwards. Removed by 1973

Inventory

The USAF inventory for the C-124 was spread from 1950 until the last was retired in 1974. The following is the official total of aircraft in service for each FY:

	1950	1951	1952	1953	1954	1955	1956	1957	1958	1959
Active duty	1	50	122	268	345	430	424	420	412	404
AFRES	-	-	-	-	-	-	-	-	-	-
ANG	-	-	-	-	-	-	-	-	-	-

	1960	1961	1962	1963	1964	1965	1966	1967	1968	1969
Active duty	401	352	398	394	375	375	293	208	187	58
AFRES	-	47	-	3	20	20	97	141	117	142
ANG	-	-	-	-	-	-	-	28	72	83

	1970	1971	1972	1973	1974
Active duty	7	7	4	3	2
AFRES	136	103	20	-	-
ANG	89	70	47	29	27

Note: the aircraft record cards are at odds with the details shown, particularly for FY 1950, which shows just one aircraft on the inventory, whereas in reality nine had been delivered, with six of these being assigned to operational units.

Above left: 909th MAG C-124A 51-0138 wearing CAC in the tail stripe for CONAC, shortly before becoming AFRES. It is at Prestwick Airport early in 1968. (Eric Roscoe)

Above right: The 374th TCW at Tachikawa initially operated its aircraft with little or no unit and Command insignia. However, by the mid-1950s, colorful markings similar to those adopted by TAC were in place, as seen on 51-0143. (Jack Friell collection)

Tempelhof Visits

The C-124 was a regular visitor to Tempelhof Airport in Berlin, resupplying the large US Army garrison, as well as other US government departments. The active duty was the primary airlifter, but as these units retired the C-124, the reserves assumed the responsibility. Presented is a selection of C-124s at the now closed Tempelhof Airport.

Above: C-124C 51-5205 about to depart Tempelhof Airport in August 1962. (Ralf Manteufel)

Left: 62nd TCW C-124C 51-7280 landing at Tempelhof Airport in November 1964. Great care had to be exercized by C-124 pilots, as the runways were only 6,000ft (1,828m) in length and surrounded by apartment blocks. (Ralf Manteufel)

Above: 63rd TCW C-124C 51-7285 making a routine resupply flight to the US sector of Berlin during September 1964. C-124s were prolific visitors to Tempelhof Airport. (Ralf Manteufel)

Right: 63rd TCW C-124C 52-0940 detached to Rhein-Main AB, landing at Tempelhof Airport past the famous apartments that were a feature of the 1948 Berlin Airlift. (Peter Seemann)

Below: An AFRES C-124C mobilized to MAC service, 51-0108 taxis in snow at Berlin's Tempelhof Airport in February 1969. (Ralf Manteufel)

Above: Oklahoma ANG 52-1037 about to taxi onto the runway at Tempelhof Airport in July 1969. (Ralf Manteufel)

Left: Making a very low approach to Tempelhof Airport, Oklahoma ANG C-124C 52-1037 passes the famous apartment blocks in July 1969. (Ralf Manteufel)

Below: Apart from active duty squadrons, the reserves also flew resupply flights to Berlin, with Oklahoma ANG C-124C 52-0998 at Tempelhof Airport in May 1971. (Peter Seemann)

Acknowledgements

Time has eroded the date when I saw my first C-124, but is was almost certainly sometime during 1958. Living at that time near RAF Northolt, Greater London, which was directly beneath the aerial artery known as airway Green One, C-124s were almost daily overflights. At an altitude of 10,000ft (3,048m), Globemasters were clearly visible on a sunny day. With Day-Glo orange applied, the sight and sound of a C-124 made a lasting impression upon this ten-year-old boy. With very rudimentary information on such matters, making notes of the serial numbers of overflying C-124s was an interesting past time. Many years later, much additional historical information on individual aircraft has become available, which has served to increase fascination with this aircraft type. Sixty-five years later, such allure remains, and has brought about this book.

The publication you are holding would not have been completed had it not been for a great many people. I am indebted to fellow enthusiasts Paul Bennett, Steve Hill, Colin Johnson, Lindsay Peacock, Chris Pocock, Geoff Rhodes, and Dave Wilton, along with numerous others whose names I have sadly forgotten. The enthusiast's "bible" *British Aviation Review* was the primary source of data, while the Air Force Historical Research Agency at Maxwell AFB was my basis for confirming the unit structures, and individual aircraft data. A host of books and magazines, which are far too numerous to list, provided valuable information. Images were sourced from many fellow photographers including Paul Bennett, Jack Friell, Jerry Geer, Steve Hill/EMCS, Steve Miller, Terry Panopalis, Kieron Pilbeam, Brian Rogers, Doug Slowiak, Nick Williams plus many others. The original photographers for the majority of images are presented after each caption. However, those where the photographer is unknown are unaccredited, and apologies are extended for this omission. I wish to thank former C-124 crew member Tony Koenig for wonderful stories and the opportunity to reminisce. Finally, I extend my gratitude to Douglas M Ducote Sr, whose C-124 Globemaster page on Facebook brings personnel associated with the type together and maintains the memory of an iconic aircraft.

63rd TCW C-124C 52-0956 on static display at RAF Bovingdon on May 14, 1960. This was the first Globemaster I had the opportunity to appreciate closely, and to scramble up the ramps to enjoy the huge internal dimensions.

52-1050 was of the 436th MAW but detached to Rhein-Main AB during the second half of 1968.

At the completion of MATS/MAC service, 51-0177 joined the 901st MAG at Hanscom AFB, and is seen visiting Mildenhall during February 1972. The aircraft was retired to MASDC six months later. (Lindsay Peacock)

A beautifully parked row of C-124Cs headed by 62nd MAW 52-0942 at MASDC during 1971. (via EMCS)

Strangely, I did not visit any C-124 bases in the US during my first visit there in 1973, and subsequent US visits were after the C-124 had been retired. Nevertheless, C-124s were frequently seen at the SAC bases during my visits between 1960 and 1964. Furthermore, Globemasters were often in transit at the USAF bases in Eastern England following my relocating to that area in 1966. Additionally, during 1968/1969, I was living in the vicinity of RAF Mildenhall during the historic mobilization of the CONAC C-124s. Without doubt, the C-124 is my favourite aircraft of all time – for no other reason than it was a slow, lumbering, awe inspiring mammoth.

The last operational sortie by a Globemaster was just shy of 50 years ago. Airlift has moved ahead in leaps and bounds, with jet-powered aircraft effortlessly spanning oceans nonstop. For C-124 crews, a Tran'sAtlantic sortie was an epic undertaking lasting ten hours or more. And at an altitude where harsh weather conditions could not be avoided. Nevertheless, Globemaster crews would not have changed one moment despite such difficulties.

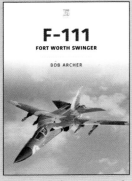

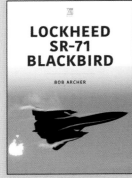
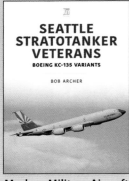

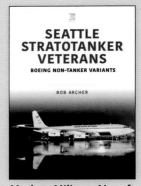